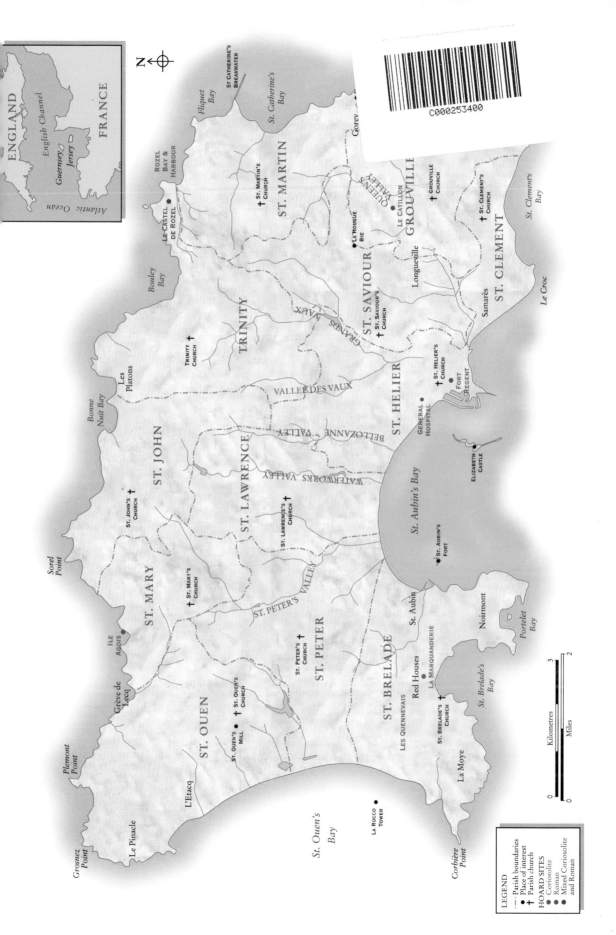

COINAGE in JERSEY

2,000 Years

D. C. Corbel, D. Gayet,
I. R. Monins and G. J. Morris

Published in 2010 by
Société Jersiaise
7 Pier Road
St Helier
Jersey   JE2 4XW

Origination by Seaflower Books, Jersey

Printed by Cromwell Press Group
Trowbridge, Wiltshire

ISBN 978-0-901897-46-6

This publication results from a concept of the late Ian Richard Monins, a former Chairman of the Numismatics Section of the Société Jersiaise, and his Section colleague the late Douglas Clarence Corbel. Their respective enthusiastic attention to detail, whilst maintaining the interest of specialist and layman alike, underlies the keen and devoted way they both approached this most interesting of subjects. It is with reflective thanks to the memory of these eloquent members in the field of numismatics in general that this work is respectfully dedicated.

CONTENTS

ACKNOWLEDGEMENTS

The Publications Committee of the Société Jersiaise, along with the several authors of the work, acknowledge with thanks UBS AG for their support and generous sponsorship of this publication.

I wish to thank all the members of the Numismatics Section for their assistance in compiling this booklet, in particular, Vernie Dougan, Geoff Morris, John Scholefield and my son Louis for their painstaking photography of the pieces illustrated.

The help of Jethro Lennox, a professional cartographer based in the UK, and his preparation of the Jersey map, was invaluable.

Finally, I would like to acknowledge all the hard work of my wife, Jill, with the typing and amendments of the draft text.

Thanks are also due to the States of Jersey Treasury for allowing us sight of the noble metal modern proofs and providing mintage details of circulating coinage. I also appreciate the input from Westminster Coin in providing details of modern coinage issues.

Daniel Gayet
Chairman of the Numismatics Section
Société Jersiaise

FOREWORD

His Excellency Lieutenant General A P Ridgway CB CBE

GOVERNMENT HOUSE
JERSEY
JE2 7GH
CHANNEL ISLANDS

The inhabitants of Jersey have been using coins as a medium of exchange for over 2,000 years and a study of our coinage provides a fascinating insight into the history of our Island. This book provides just such an insight. It is a work of considerable scholarship being based on detailed research and analysis by the authors, all members of the highly respected Numismatics Section of the Société Jersiaise. Despite being a work of scholarship of considerable interest to those with a passion for ancient coins, it is much more than that. It provides a riveting account of the part that coins have played in the development of the community in our Island over the centuries, and will be of great interest to anyone with a desire to obtain a better understanding of the history of Jersey.

The book charts the development of the use of coins from the earliest Celtic times, when it would appear that wealthy Celtic individuals used the safety of the Island as a haven in which to hide their funds: something that would be impossible in today's closely regulated financial climate! The international nature of the Island's community is a recurring theme throughout the book! The many finds of Roman coins are well documented despite continuing question marks about the extent, if any, of Roman occupation of the Island. Similarly the Medieval period is smattered with finds of coins emanating widely from across Europe, including from Portugal, thus providing a precursor to the current Portuguese contribution to Jersey's economy.

Inevitably, French coinage is very much in evidence right across the post-medieval period suggesting that trade continued even during periods of conflict. I was particularly interested to learn that plans for the creation of Jersey's first Mint, to be built in Trinity, were developed during the English Civil War when Prince Charles had no access to English funds. The building of the Mint was probably overtaken by the Cromwellian invasion of 1651 and it is interesting to note that it was only in 1834 that English money became the only legal tender. How history turns full circle now that the Euro is widely accepted in the Island.

For me one of the most interesting sections in the book concerns the issue, or rather non-issue, of base metal Tokens by the German Forces during the occupation. These tokens are extremely authentic and provided access to the various *Soldatenheims* and could have been used in exchange for milk and bread and other commodities. However, no such tokens were ever actually issued at the time. Nonetheless, they can be purchased widely on the Internet today having been struck in California where they have become very collectable!

The story of the development of coinage in the Isand is beautifully illustrated throughout this excellent book. I commend it to anyone with a real interest in the history of our Island and I congratulate the authors for producing such a readable account of a highly technical subject.

PREFACE

This publication is not intended to be an exhaustive catalogue for all Jersey coins but rather an outline of the history of our coinage, with particular reference to local finds both singly and hoards.

The work has been undertaken by the active members of the Numismatics Section of the Société Jersiaise who have contributed by way of compiling chapters relating to their own particular interests. Much new material has come to us for examination in recent years, mainly from casual finds on demolition sites and metal detecting on beaches and fields with the farmer's permission by the Jersey Detector Club who kindly show us their finds for identification and recording.

On a historical note, Jersey has been a possession of the British Crown since it was part of the Dukedom of Normandy. It is thought that the ancestors of some Jerseymen fought with the army of Duke William in his conquest of England in October 1066, after which he is usually known as William the Conqueror. When Normandy was lost during the reign of King John, Jersey decided to remain loyal to the English Crown and, in return, the Island was granted various privileges and rights. This is the main reason why the Island is today part of the British Isles but not part of the United Kingdom.

Due to the close proximity of France, by far the most coinage circulating originated from France until recent times. French bronze coins ceased to be legal tender in 1887 here, whilst the silver circulated in the Island right up until after the First World War. As the reader will discover, other coinage was brought in and must have been accepted at different times until the Island finally developed its own during the nineteenth century.

Bank notes were issued in Jersey from the end of the eighteenth century. These are considered to be a separate subject outside the scope of this book, with the exception of the issues during the Second World War as no metal was available for mintage.

The Numismatics Section wishes to correct two well-known errors consistently reported in various publications. Firstly, the numbers of three shilling and eighteen pence silver tokens of 1813 struck were 71,000 and 38,740, respectively, and not the reverse. Secondly, the 1844 1/13th of a shilling usually has a recorded total of 27,400. This should, in fact, be 145,600.

Finally, it is hoped that this booklet will be of interest both to locals and visitors to the Island.

I THE CORIOSOLITES

Around 300BC a Celtic tribe named the Coriosolites became dominant in the area of mainland France to the south of Jersey in part of modern-day Brittany and Normandy. It is thought by some that Jersey became part of their empire but by others that the Island was used by the tribe as an off-shore haven because most of the finds here have been in medium to large hoards, although there have been some single finds as well.

One of the earliest coin series struck by Philip II of Macedon in the 4th Century BC had an obverse showing the head of Apollo whilst the reverse pictured a *biga* (chariot) with driver being pulled by two galloping horses. These coins gradually spread round the known world in the course of trade and were widely copied by the Celts. As the years passed by copies of copies were struck and adapted by each tribe with its own particular stylised form of art. A study of all the tribes of Armorica (north-west France) will reveal striking similarities in the artistic style.

Whilst the surrounding tribes had coinages predominantly in silver with some gold, the Coriosolites issued billon pieces consisting of an alloy of mainly silver and copper. All the coins struck around 75-50 BC were mute (without inscription) and fall into six classes. Rather curiously, when struck the dies used appear to have always been larger than the flans for both obverse and reverse. Consequently, one has to examine quite a number of pieces to obtain the complete picture which includes numerous marked variations in style.

Most classes are also represented in much smaller versions known as quarter staters, also in billon. These do not turn up very frequently and exist in the ratio of less than one to a hundred full staters. In the author's opinion they are somewhat undervalued in catalogues as specimens are much more difficult to obtain than full size versions.

Over sixteen thousand Coriosolite coins have been found in Jersey, including the largest hoard containing around eleven to twelve thousand staters discovered in April 1935 at La Marquanderie, St Brelade, whilst digging the foundations for a house.

I list below the hoards discovered to date in order:

Date	Site	Contents of hoard
1787	Fort Regent	Not known but Gaulish including Coriosolite
1795	'Near the great harbour, Jersey'	Not known but Gaulish including Coriosolite
1807	Near Rozel Harbour	Gaulish, including some Coriosolite and possibly one coin each of the Unelli and Osismii tribes
1820	Coastal cliff fall, area unknown	982 Armorican coins, nearly all Coriosolite, a few Unelli, Baiocasses and uncertain tribes
1875	Le Castel de Rozel	About 1,000 Gaulish coins, including Coriosolite; also around 20 Roman silver denarii
1883	Rozel	Not recorded, but included Gaulish and Roman coins
c.1897	Rozel	Over 200 Gaulish coins, probably including Coriosolite
1935	La Marquanderie, St. Brelade	Between 11,000 and 12,000 coins, nearly all Coriosolite with a handful of other Gaulish tribes
1957/1959	Le Catillon, Grouville	Around 2,500 coins in total. 2,228 and 41 were Coriosolite staters and quarter staters, respectively; also included were 21 British (of which 19 Durotiges). Amongst the hoard was the gold stater of the Biocasses tribe (see picture on front cover)

It is thought that these hoards were all buried during the second half of the 1st Century BC, and it probably follows that Jersey was occupied by the Coriosolites at that time. Did they move here from mainland France and bury their riches whilst escaping their Roman pursuers after losing their lands during Rome's conquest of Gaul? This has been the subject of much discussion over the years and will probably never be satisfactorily explained as no records of any kind have ever been found (unlike the Romans) as the Celts had no written language.

Let us now turn our attention to the design of the coins. I shall classify these according to Spink's *Standard Catalogue of British Coins,* in which they can be found under reference numbers 14-20 inclusive.

No. 14 – class I

Obverse: head right with closed eye.

Reverse: horse galloping right, boar below, part of driver with victory above. Driver has lash ending in two loops or a gate, mostly with a pattern rather like the union flag.

No. 15 – class II

Obverse: head right.

Reverse: horse galloping right, boar below, no driver, remains of victory above. Driver has lash ending in cross of four pellets.

No. 16 - class III

Obverse: head right with nose resembling an anchor.

Reverse: similar to No. 14.

No. 17 – class IV

Obverse: head right – the most unrealistic looking one of them all.

Reverse: horse galloping right with reins, shape under the horse believed to be either representation of a lyre or Halley's Comet. Driver holds a pole with disc at the top and has lash ending in three prongs.

No. 18 – class V

Similar to No. 17 but lash ends in large cross with pellets (sometimes no lash).

No. 19 – class VI

Again, similar to No. 17 but lash ends in a ladder-shape, and boar under horse instead of lyre.

diam. 22mm   diam. 9mm
These are examples of a Class 2 full stater and a class 4 quarter stater

No. 20 – Quarter stater
Types as above.

It should be pointed out that the above descriptions of nos. 14 to 19 are broad and many different dies are known.

Class II (No. 15) is by far the most common type, whether found in hoards or singly. It is thought that the order of issue of the above was 17, 18 and 19 together, then 14, 16 and 15. It has also been observed that on analysis of the metal content the earlier issues contain a higher proportion of silver.

Corrosion is a problem with all these coins and they are frequently found encrusted in verdigris and brown deposits, and quite often stuck together when discovered in hoards. Not surprisingly, most examples have been cleaned when die study is contemplated. The rarity of the quarter staters is not helped in that it is very difficult to obtain a good example as corrosion usually affects these pieces quite badly due to their small diameter and thickness in comparison with the full size staters.

Various interested parties have at different times undertaken studies of the Coriosolite coinage and suggested re-classifications therein. It is felt that detailed study of this is beyond the scope of this booklet but the reader is invited to see the list of suggested further reading at the end of this publication if he wishes to pursue this further.

Since this chapter was written, the conclusions of John Hooker have become available (see Select Bibliography). He considers that the last Coriosolite issue (Rybot II) was probably struck by the Unelli. He also suggests the deposit of the Le Catillon hoard to a date long after the Gallic War, possibly as late as the revolt *circa* 10-15AD. If this is correct, it means that the dating of the British coins in that hoard must be revised.

II THE ROMANS

There is at present no evidence to show that the Romans inhabited Jersey for a protracted period. The only confirmed sites that are known are a small Roman building at the Pinnacle Rock at the northern end of St Ouen's Bay, and the immediate area around St Clement's Church which has produced pottery and a few late bronze coins in poor condition. Some Roman pottery fragments have also been found in St Helier and elsewhere in St Ouen. The inhabitants may, in fact, have been Celts living in a partly Roman style copied from that of mainland France.

Several hoards have, however, been discovered in the Island over the years. These are listed below in order:

Date	Site	Contents of hoard
1875	Le Castel de Rozel	18 Republican silver denarii and 2 bronzes found with the hoard of Gaulish coins (see previous chapter) c.145-10BC
1974-5	Ile Agois, St Mary	18 bronze antoniniani c. 253-268AD
1848	Les Quennevais	Over 400 bronze coins c. 284-361AD
1973	General Hospital, St Helier (during building excavations)	12 bronze coins c. 337-390AD

Interestingly, all the above finds have been on or within a short distance from the coast. This could suggest that the Island was passed on the known trade route between northern France and Hengistbury Head in Hampshire.

Detailed recording of the first hoard above is as follows (all denarii except 18/19):

1 Head of Roma, X behind R/Diana in biga, ROMA below 145-138BC (Sydenham 736)

2 P. Maenius Antiatitus 119-110BC (Sydenham 492)
3 Identical coin to 2. Above.
4 M. Sergius Silus 109-108BC (Sydenham 544)
5 Appius Claudius and Titus Mallius 106BC (Sydenham 570)
6 Uncertain but probably A. Postumius Albinius 92-91BC (Sydenham 612)
7 L. Titurius L.f. Sabinus 88BC (Sydenham 698)
8 C. Licinius L.f. Macer 83BC (Sydenham 732)
9 C. Postumius 74-73BC (Sydenham 785)
10 M. Aemilius Scaurus and P. Plautius Hypsaeus 58BC (Sydenham 913)
11 L. Scribonius Libo 55BC (Sydenham 928)
12 Q. Cassius Longinus 76BC or L. Cassius Longinus 52-50BC (Sydenham 935)
13 P. Clodius 41BC (Sydenham 1117)
14 Marcus Antonius and Octavianus 40-39BC
15)
16 Marcus Antonius (3 examples including a legionary issue)
17)
18 Two copper asses of Ceasar Augustus c.10BC
19)
20 Bronze sestertius of Trajan Decius c.250AD probably an intruder (i.e. found at the same time but not thought to relate to the hoard due to being struck in a quite different period).

The second hoard was discovered during excavation work by the Société Jersiaise and was recorded as shown:-

Emperor	Reign	Mint						
		Antioch	Cologne	Lugdunum	Mediolanum	Rome	Uncertain	Total
Valerian I	253-260AD	1				2		3
Gallienus	253-268AD			1	1	2	2	6
Salonina	268AD					1		1
Postumus	259-268AD		7	1				8
Total		1	7	2	1	5	2	18

In addition, an unusual example of a barbarous radiate of Postumus was found nearby at the same time – see overleaf.

The third hoard from Les Quennevais is the largest Roman one found in Jersey to date. In 1922, the British Museum examined 357 of the coins and their analysis is shown at the end of this chapter.

The last hoard consists of coins struck in the second half of the fourth century and ranges from an *Urbs Roma* commemorative to the reign of Theodosius I, 379-395AD, and Eastern mints are the more numerous.

Over the years, and in particular since the advent of metal detectors, odd Roman coins have been found both in fields and on beaches. There are, however, no recorded finds in this context from the fifth century, as far as is known to the author. This would suggest that Roman influence affected the Island in a limited way after the conquest of Britain and Gaul, but there was not much activity here possibly because the Island was too small and the fall of the Empire probably had little effect on the day to day life of the inhabitants.

Single coin finds in Jersey brought in for identification include Roman and are recorded each year in the Numismatics Section report of the Société Jersiaise *Bulletin*. No conclusions can really be made from the four hoards and the odd coin finds so far all relating to the Roman period. It is hoped that as time passes more material will come to light, thus providing further clues as to the life-style at this time amongst the inhabitants and whether the coinage was in daily use.

Examples from Les Quennevais Hoard:

A E Follis – Maximianus
second reign 306-308AD
DE MAXIMIANV(S) PFS AVG
R/GENIO POP ROMANI
PLN (London) mint
diam. 25mm approx

A E Follis – Licinius I 308-324AD
IMP LICINIVS PF AVG
R/GENIO POP ROM
 ATR (Treveri) mint
diam. 20mm approx

A E Follis – Constantine I 307-337AD
IMP CONSTANTINVS AVG
R/SOLI INVICTO COMITI
ATR (Treveri) mint
diam. 20mm approx

EMPEROR	REIGN	MINT												
		Arelate	Cyzicus	Heraclea	Londinium	Lugdunum	Ostia	Rome	Siscia	Thessalonica	Ticinum	Treveri	Uncertain	Total
Diocletian	284-305AD												1	1
Maximianus	286-310AD				6						1		3	10
Constantius I	305-306AD				7						1	2	1	11
Galerius	305-311AD								1			4	1	6
Maximinius II	309-313AD				5					1		11		17
Maxentius	306-312AD							4			4		3	11
Licinius I	308-324AD	5		1	32		2		2		1	42		85
Constantine I	307-337AD	23			86	23	4	4		1	9	39	17	206
Crispus	317-326AD		1											1
Constantine II	337-340AD												1	1
'Constantinopolis' commemorative	330-346AD												1	1
Constantius II	337-361AD		1					1					1	3
Uncertain													4	4
Total		28	2	1	136	23	6	9	3	2	16	98	33	357

It can be seen that Western European mints are more common above as opposed to Eastern ones

III   MEDIAEVAL

For the first half of the period covered by this chapter Jersey has little known history, even less than for the earlier centuries when slight evidence of Roman influences have been discovered. Some local place names seem to have originated from sporadic visits of the Norsemen but no Viking coins have been found in Jersey; the only numismatic legacy from these times is the small hoard of Carolingian deniers found on the Ile Agois, off St Mary.

Charles the Bald, 840-877AD. silver denier – mint of Melle. diam. 20mm

The earliest years of the Duchy of Normandy are scantily documented, but by the eleventh century there is evidence of a settled population in the Island, with ecclesiastical and feudal political structures based on the similar institutions in Normandy, to which dues were paid. It would seem that such remittances were effected mostly in kind rather than coin or bullion.

An extensive coinage was struck by the Duke of Normandy at Rouen, but none have been found in Jersey.

Richard, 943-996AD. Feudal France, Normandy. silver denier. diam. 20mm

Alphonse of France, 1185-1209AD. Silver denier. diam. 19mm

However, a base silver denier of Anjou attributed to the early years of the twelfth century was recently discovered, attributed to Foulques V (1109-1129), Count of Anjou (Boudeau 153). These deniers circulated extensively in Normandy.

Foulques V Anjou. Silver denier. diam. 19mm

There is little evidence of English coinage in Jersey while the Island was still part of Normandy, but a half-penny (actually a penny cut in half) of Henry II, struck at York c.1180, has been found on a mediaeval site in St Helier.

John 1199-1216AD. Cut silver halfpenny class 5b
mint mark crosspatee – moneyer Beneit on Lynde (London)
diam. 18mm (of full penny)

Thus while there is historical evidence than when Jersey was part of the Duchy of Normandy coinage was known, so little has survived that it is difficult to believe that it was in everyday use among the inhabitants, whose subsistence economy would have had little need of it.

There were changes after the political separation of Jersey from Normandy in 1204, although the Island continued to be linked to France as far as the Church was concerned. A significant factor was the new fortifications at Gorey Castle. Some of the expenses of construction and payment of a garrison from outside the Island may have been paid in kind, but for much of local numismatics history since the separation from Normandy, the Castle has been the main source of evidence.

An early example from the Castle is a denier of Arthur II of Brittany (1305-1312) (cf Boudeau 47).

Arthur I Bretagne 1180-1206AD silver denier. diam. 19mm

Other French coins found there include double parisis and tournois of Philippe VI (Ciani 313 and 319), and an anonymous provincial denier of Chartres (cf. Boudeau 204).

It may be remarked that in mediaeval France two distinct monetary systems evolved, the "Parisis" and the "Tournois", the latter eventually superseding the former. As a money of account, 12 deniers (pence) = 1 sol (shilling), and 20 sols = 1 pound, the Tournois system survived in Jersey well into the XIX century, although by then the "Livre Tournois" was worth far less then the British Pound Sterling.

Philippe VI 1346AD silver double parisis. diam. 23mm

Anglo-Gallic coins are represented by a groat of Edward, "the Black Prince" from Aquitaine (Boudeau 509), a hardi of Henry IV, also from Aquitaine, and a demi-leopard of Henry V minted at St Lo (Duplessey 442).

Edward I silver denier or leopard of Aquitaine. diam. 20mm

Henry IV 1399-1453 silver hardi. diam. 19mm

English Edwardian halfpennies have been found at the Castle; more unexpected was a Portuguese dinhero of Alfonso III (1248-1279).

Edward I 1292-1307 silver halfpenny. diam. 15mm

A few other mediaeval coins have been found in other parts of the Island, in particular a gold quarter-noble of Edward III. Also, a recent find at La Rocque was a gold Florin of John of Luxembourg (1310-1346) of Bohemia (Katz 24, cf. Saumur 394, 395).

Edward III 1327-1377 silver penny
3rd or florin coinage of York. diam. 19mm

John the Blind 1309-1346 silver sterling. diam. 17mm.

A short-cross cut-halfpenny was found at Le Catel, Trinity, and a penny of Edward III near Côtes-du-Nord, Trinity. A feudal denier of Alphonse de France (1249-1271) of Provence was found at La Moye, St Brelade; a fragment of a denier, probably of Louis VIII, in St Helier, a billon double of Jean II (Ciani 433) from St Brelade's churchyard, and a denier tournois of Charles VIII (cf Ciani 835) near St Clement's Church.

In the absence of hoards, the casual losses of stray coins mentioned above gives an incomplete picture of coinage circulating in Jersey in mediaeval times. English coins seem to have been rare before the separation of the Island from Normandy, and proof of intensive everyday use of coins is lacking.

After 1204, more English coins seem to have reached the Island, although French still predominated. The English quarter-noble is exceptional as a high value piece recovered. A groat of Henry VI and a half-groat of Henry VII have recently been discovered at St Peter and Grouville respectively.

Henry VI 1422-1461 Silver groat of Calais (Annulet Issue 1422-1427). diam. 26mm.

It may be suggested that the more valuable coins which reached the Island left it to pay for imports; recorded finds are mostly only petty coins. Nevertheless the latter indicate that a variety of coins did reach Jersey, but with present knowledge it is impossible to make a reasonable estimate of the quantity of coinage in the Island during the Middle Ages, or how or to what extent it circulated. Jersey had enough inhabitants to support twelve parish churches , and it is disappointing that so little numismatic evidence has been left for posterity. There are surviving documentary records of payments; taxes, fines, commercial transactions, for fortifications and to garrisons; but although sums of money may be specified, the exact methods of settlements remain uncertain.

IV POST-MEDIAEVAL TO
THE FRENCH REVOLUTION

The beginning of the XVI century is a convenient point to commence consideration of the post-mediaeval development of the use of coinage in Jersey. The great political, religious and economic upheavals of this century, if not immediately, eventually had their effects on the life of the islanders and their financial affairs.

There are now more references in surviving documents to monetary matters. But finds of XVI century coins in the island are still far from numerous; rarely are higher value pieces, either English or Continental, mentioned in connection with fiscal and commercial affairs.

Gorey Castle has yielded a few English Tudor silver coins; a groat of Henry VIII (three quarter facing bust), a base silver penny of Edward VI and Philip and Mary (the latter minted at York for issue in Ireland), and a sixpence of Elizabeth. These coins are from the period when the castle was being enlarged and refortified, and there is a lack of similar finds from other parts of the island to give evidence that such coins were in general circulation among the local population.

Francois I 1515-1547 silver douzain. diam. 26mm

Elizabeth I fifth issue silver 6d of 1599 mint-mark anchor. diam. 26mm

France Charles IX 1560-74 silver teston of 1563. M=Toulouse. diam. 32 mm

As far as French currency is concerned, the castle has also given up a few XVI century coins; douzains of Louis XII and Francois I; also a number of base "Deniers à l'Hermine", presumably counterfeit copies of the deniers issued by Louis XII for circulation in Brittany. Other French coins of this century have been found elsewhere in Jersey, in particular a douzain of Charles X (posthumous) at St Ouen.

Charles X 1589-1590 silver douzain. diam. 25mm

Finds of coins from the time of Henri IV, at the end of the century, include a silver quart d'ecu from Gorey Castle, another from St Clement, and a third from Samarès.

Henry IV silver 1/4 ecu of 1602. diam. 30mm

French XVI century feudal or provincial coins found in Jersey include issues of Antoine & Jeanne of Navarre, and the Comtant-Venaissin from Gorey Castle, and another of the Comtant-Venaissin from La Moye.

In general, reported finds of XVI century coins are insufficient to give a very satisfactory idea of what was then circulating in the Island. Any gold or silver of high value, which came to Jersey, seems to have continued to be sent out of the Island, in view of the absence of hoards and scarcity of single finds. An exceptional find has been a gold escudo of Philip IV from the beach at St Aubin's Bay.

The record of numismatic finds changes dramatically in the XVII century as far as copper coinage is concerned. The Doubles Tournois of Louis XIII and the Liards of Louis XIV are found in the fields and beaches of the Island in abundance. The critical problem is the time when such coins reached Jersey and came into common circulation. Most such coins are found in very poor condition; apart from the effect of the time spent in the ground or the sands of the sea, they must have suffered considerable circulation wear.

Louis XIII 1610-1643 copper double tournois. diam. 20mm

Louis XIV 1643-1715 copper liard de France. diam. 24mm

Louis XIV 1643-1715 copper liard de France. diam. 24mm

They include some counterfeits and coins of the remaining feudal states such as Dombes, Rethel and Sedan. It seems likely that these insignificant pieces were shipped in quantity from France to Jersey, presumably at a profit to the exporter, when they became unacceptable in France. If this hypothesis is correct, they arrived in Jersey many years after they had been issued in France.

Gaston D'Orleans 1627-1650 copper denier of Dombes. diam. 17mm

Louis XIV silver 1/12 ecu of 1648. diam. 20mm

Charles II De Gonzague 1637-1659 copper denier of Rethel. diam. 17mm

In mid-century, the English Civil War, the visits of Prince Charles to Jersey, and increased interference by the Commonwealth government in local affairs brought the Island into much closer links with England. Historical records surviving are considerable, but numismatic evidence is scanty. It is significant that precious metal "Civil War hoards", so many of which have been recovered in England, are absent from Jersey, a further indication that there was still little high value coinage in the hands of most of the inhabitants.

The numerous entourages of Prince Charles were not so wealthy as to have brought much money with them; and such funds as they had would have been needed to obtain supplies from France. Their rather impecunious position leads to a consideration of the "Jersey Mint".

There is no doubt that following precedents of the Court of Charles I in establishing mints as it needed to relocate according to the viscitudes of war, there was an intention to set up a mint in Jersey. Surviving documents substantiate this fact, and premises for a mint were arranged at La Guerdainerie, Trinity. But its subsequent history is uncertain. If coins were actually produced there, no survivors have been identified in Jersey or elsewhere. It has been suggested that dies that had been used at some English mint could have been utilised, and the whole output sent out of the Island. Even so, supplies of bullion must have been scanty and output small. Or were counterfeit coins struck? The Jersey mint remains enigmatic.

Although so much French copper from the latter part of the XVII century has survived, finds of precious metal coinage of this period are rare. In 1658 the liard was devalued in France from three to two deniers, that is, six liards to the sol instead of four. In Jersey, however, the liard continued to be valued at three deniers, still four to the sol. There was therefore even more encouragement to send these liards to Jersey, rather than remit payment from France in silver; the copper was worth half as much again in Jersey as in France.

The States of Jersey appreciated the position, but with these insignificant coins the staple currency of the Island, and with the inhabitants holding their savings in them due to the lack of better money, hesitated to take action until 1714, when they prohibited the import of more than 120 of these coins. In the event, this law proved impossible to enforce. In 1729 an official devaluation of them from four to six liards to the sol led to civil disturbance. The new law was largely ignored, and for their own purposes Jerseymen continued to consider the liards as four to the sol.

More numismatic evidence from finds of XVIII century coins gradually gives a clearer picture of coinage in circulation in the Island. After the financial troubles in France at the end of the reign of Louis XIV, and the early years of Louis XV, that country enjoyed a stable currency until the end of the century and the Revolution. Trade between Jersey and France was increasing, likewise with England; Jersey ships were voyaging further, in particular in connection with the Newfoundland cod trade.

Naturally, such trade would be facilitated by the availability of high value coins as and when available. As in previous centuries what was received for exports was needed to pay for imports. But there was so often a shortage of gold and silver that in 1701 and 1720 the States of Jersey placed restrictions on the export of gold and silver; there can have been little other than the liards in the hands of most of the inhabitants. However, a gold Louis d'or of Louis XIV, 1691.B (Rouen) (Duplessey 1435A) was recently found on the beach in St Aubin's Bay. This coin is of particular numismatic interest as it is overstruck on an earlier coin of Louis XIII 1641 A (Paris) (Duplessey 1298).

Numismatic finds are still mainly French, although English coppers appear as the century progressed; British troops who came to garrison the Island must have brought some of the latter. Quite a number of coins from more distant parts, particularly Spain and Portugal, are evidence of expanding maritime activity.

Gradually more French silver coinage appears; at first low denominations, but towards the end of the century higher values, including large ecus. The liards continue to predominate in finds, with a few Louis XV coppers, but much more frequently those of Louis XVI, both his earlier issues and those of the constitutional period immediately before the Revolution. All these coppers continued to circulate well into the XIX century, at least until Jersey had its own copper coinage in 1841. There is a lack of hoard evidence; but it seems certain that as in previous times, French coinage continued to arrive in the Island a long time after it had been issued, or even had ceased to be acceptable in France.

Louis XVI 1774-1793 Louis d'Or. diam. 24mm

In spite of the wars between Great Britain and France, considerable trade usually continued between Jersey and France; and reductions in trade from periodic disruptions was more than compensated for by the profits of extensive privateering. Jersey was now prosperous.

Louis XVI copper sol of 1791. W = Lille Mint. diam. 28-30mm

Louis XVI silver Ecu aux Lavriers of 1785. I = Limoges mint. diam. 41mm

Yet there is evidence that with an increasing local market economy, there was a shortage of coin in the hands of the inhabitants, causing much inconvenience. This is illustrated by an advertisement in 1787, when the public was asked to bring the necessary small change when collecting and paying for letters! The overall coinage situation was still far from satisfactory, and continued so until well into the next century.

V JERSEY MODERN COINAGE

The Napoleonic wars disrupted trade with France, the major source of Jersey's coinage in use for everyday transactions. The most urgent shortage was the absence of the 24, 12 and 6 sol coins which had been used as 2/-, 1/- and 6d pieces especially as many of these had been bought by Guernsey merchants from Jersey at a premium to meet their own deficiency. The States of Jersey passed an Act to issue local coins of Three Shillings and Eighteen Pence, approved by the Privy Council provided that they were struck at the Royal Mint as 'tokens' from silver supplied by Jersey. In March and June 1813 and February 1814 approximately 71,100 Three Shilling Tokens and 38,740 Eighteen Pence Tokens were struck.

1813
Three shilling silver token
diam. 34.95mm

1813
Eighteen pence silver token
diam. 26.5mm

Meanwhile Jersey business houses had begun to issue their own notes for one pound and even five shillings and two shillings & sixpence and copper tokens for One Penny and for a Halfpenny appeared which may have been brought in by such traders. The silver 'token' issues were welcomed and the issue of notes of less value than one pound sterling forbidden. These tokens were hoarded, despite being of less intrinsic value than their denomination, and became scarce. They were withdrawn in 1834 when only English money became legal tender in Jersey.

Druid head
copper one penny
Undated
diam. 33.5mm

Prince of Wales
copper one penny
1813
diam. 33.5mm

The French liards and similar foreign coins which were in use as small change had become scarce and badly worn so the States of Jersey passed an Act on 13th July 1840 to issue £1,000 worth of copper coins, subject to the approval of Her Majesty Queen Victoria in Council. These were to be in denominations of 1/13th, 1/26th and 1/52nd of a shilling in an attempt to relate British sterling to the previously current French coinage, similar to the introduction of the Euro coin of today, the halfpenny being equal to a sou or 1/26th of a shilling. Half the coins were 1/26ths, being the successor to the sou, and the other half was split equally beween the 1/13ths and 1/52nds.

Victoria
1841 copper issue
1/13 of a shilling
diam. 34.5mm

1841 copper issue
1/26 of a shilling
diam. 28.1mm

1841 copper issue
1/52 of a shilling
diam. 21.9mm

In 1844 these were supplemented by an issue of the same amount of 1/26ths and 145,600 1/13ths, not the 27,400 1/13ths often recorded. All Jersey mintages are low, in comparison with other countries, yet still readily available for collectors at reasonable prices.

In 1866 a new smaller bronze coinage, bearing a coronetted head of Queen Victoria, was issued in 1/13ths and 1/26ths.

1866 bronze
1/13 small size issue
diam. 29.35mm

1866 bronze
1/26 small size issue
diam. 24.25mm

Jersey traders found it complicated to have to deal in English and Jersey pennies of different values and petitioned the States resulting in an Act changing the denominations to 1/12th, 1/24th and 1/48th of a shilling. This new coinage, dated 1877 with a larger head on the obverse and with the date on the reverse as well as a heater-shaped shield, was struck, by arrangement with the Royal Mint who were committed for other work, by R. Heaton & Son of Birmingham. It is the only issue to bear an H under the Queen's truncated head.

1877 bronze
1/12 of a shilling
diam. 30.7mm

1877 bronze
1/24 of a shilling
diam. 25.55mm

1877 bronze
1/48 of a shilling
diam. 20.3mm

Coins were struck when they were needed in the denominations required. The next major change took place in the penultimate year of the reign of Edward VII when the new obverse bore the King's head. These 1/12ths and 1/24ths are the only Jersey coins struck during his reign. Some of the old coinage was returned to the Mint for melting to be used for this new issue which may account for the streaky appearance of some of these coins.

Edward VII
1909 bronze
1/12 of a shilling
diam. 30.85mm

Edward VII
1909 bronze
1/24 of a shilling
diam. 25.55mm

More coins were required in 1911 and these had a new obverse bearing the crowned bust of George V by Edgar Bertram Mackennal.

George V
1911 bronze
1/12 of a shilling
diam. 30.9mm

George V
1911 bronze
1/24 of a shilling
diam. 25.55mm

The year 1923 saw two issues of 1/12ths and 1/24ths the second of which had a new reverse by George Edward Kruger Gray with a squarer shield and the legends on a ribbon.

George V 1923 bronze 1/12 of a shilling.
diam. 30.8mm

George V 1923 bronze 1/24 of a shilling.
diam. 25.5mm

In 1931 a more modern reverse by Kruger Gray was introduced on both denominations which removed the ribbons resulting in a simpler design.

George V
1931 bronze
1/12 of a shilling
diam. 30.8mm

George V
1931 bronze
1/24 of a shilling
diam. 25.5mm

1937 saw the first issue of Jersey coins to bear Percy Metcalfe's crowned bust of George VI on the 1/12ths and the 1/24ths.

George VI
1937 bronze
1/12 of a shilling
diam. 30.8mm

George VI
1937 bronze
1/24 of a shilling
diam. 25.5mm

This was the last issue before the German Occupation of the Island from 1940 to 1945 during which period German Reichspfennigs circulated along with other coins.

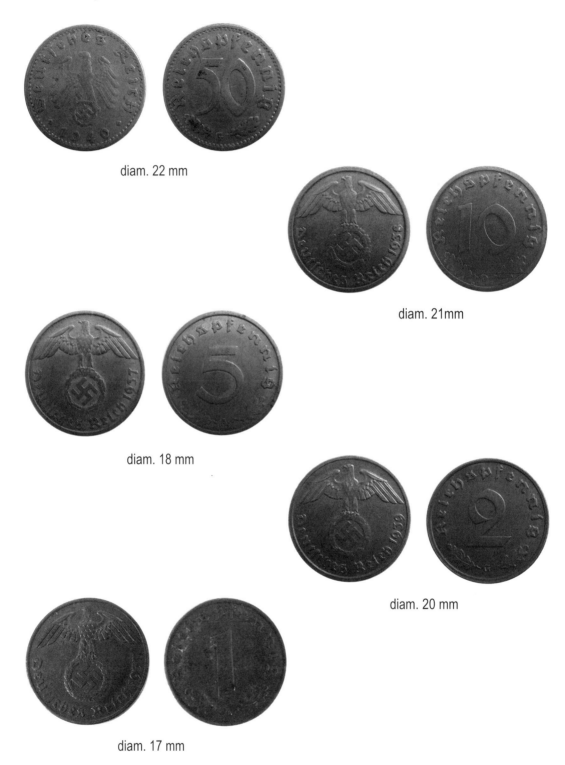

diam. 22 mm

diam. 21mm

diam. 18 mm

diam. 20 mm

diam. 17 mm

Examples of German coins of zinc and brass in circulation 1940-1945

Examples of German banknotes in circulation 1940-1945

The States of Jersey issued notes in denominations of sixpence, one, two and ten shillings and one pound to provide currency for trade (see page 75).

After the German Occupation the coinage of George VI resumed with the issues of 1946 and 1947 in both 1/12ths and 1/24ths.

George VI
1947 bronze
1/12 of a shilling
diam. 30.8mm

George VI
1946 bronze
1/24 of a shilling
diam. 25.5mm

There then occurred the issue of a commemorative 1/12th on which the only date to be seen is that in the reverse legend Liberated 1945 and Island of Jersey is substituted for the previously used States of Jersey. This was at the instigation of J. Wilfrid du Pre and was minted in the years 1949, 1950 and 1952.

The first issue under the reign of Queen Elizabeth II in 1954 bore the crowned bust of Her Majesty with a simplified legend starting clockwise from her crown on the new obverse. The reverse remained that of George VI's Liberated 1945 thus puzzling the unwary with a date prior to her coronation.

George VI
1945 bronze
1/12 of a shilling
diam. 30.8mm

Elizabeth II
1945 bronze
1/12 of a shilling
diam. 30.8mm

The second issue, in 1957, when only 1/12ths were struck, although now joined by a round nickel-brass 1/4th of a shilling, had an altered obverse with legend appearing clockwise from the lower left of the bust and the reverse legend now read Bailiwick of Jersey.

Elizabeth II
1957 bronze
1/12 of a shilling
diam. 30.8mm

Elizabeth II
1957 nickel-brass
1/4 of a shilling
diam. 21.05mm

In 1960 a 1/12th was struck to commemorate the restoration of Charles II who had sought refuge in Jersey during the rule of Cromwell and the Commonwealth. The reverse had CIIR 1660-1960 EIIR under the shield. A round 1/4 of a shilling was also struck but only for proof sets, not for circulation.

Elizabeth II
1660-1960 bronze
1/12 of a shilling
diam. 30.8mm

In 1964 a new twelve sided 1/4th of a shilling accompanied the issue of 1/12ths and this was for general use.

Elizabeth II
1964 nickel-brass
1/4 of a shilling
diam. 21.1.mm

Elizabeth II
1964 bronze
1/12 of a shilling
diam. 30.8mm

1966 saw the issue of a new commemorative issue to record 900 years of Norman Conquest when William the Conqueror, already possessing Jersey, seized the throne of England. The reverses of the 1/12th, the 1/4 of a shilling and the first introduction of a Five Shilling coin in cupro-nickel had 1066 to the left of the shield and 1966 to the right.

cupro-nickel
diam. 38.6mm

bronze
diam. 30.8mm

nickel-brass
diam. 21.15mm

The decimalisation of U.K. coins made it necessary for Jersey to issue its own new coinage and it was decided that all denominations, in line with those of the U.K., should be struck. The first coins, bearing the date 1968, were the five and ten New Pence which had a new crowned bust of Queen Elizabeth II by Arnold Machin and the reverses were inscribed with the new denominations. The old shilling and florin were to continue in this form.

cupro-nickel
diam 28.50mm

cupro-nickel
diam. 23.6mm

In 1969 a seven sided fifty pence piece in cupro-nickel was issued also inscribed as New Pence.

diam. 30.00mm

1971 saw the introduction of the new size of halfpenny, penny and twopence coins each having their denominations described as New Pence. The decimal formats were in place.

45

bronze
diam. 17.25mm

bronze
diam. 20.30mm

bronze
diam. 25.95mm

An issue to commemorate Her Majesty's Silver Wedding took place in 1972, struck by York Stampings Limited of Birmingham. This consisted of four silver and five gold coins all bearing an obverse of Arnold Machin's bust of the Queen with the legend Queen Elizabeth II – Silver Wedding 1972. The silver coins had on their reverse Bailiwick of Jersey and the denominations with differing designs. The small, round, fifty pence had the royal mace of Jersey superimposed on an outline of the Island; the larger one pound showed three florets of the Jersey Lily; the double florin sized two pounds depicted the Jersey sailing ship Alexandra; the crown sized two pounds fifty pence bore a lobster. The gold coins continued with the same obverse and reverse legends with distictive designs. The very small five pounds displayed a lesser white toothed shrew; the slightly larger ten pounds had a Bronze Age gold torque found in Jersey and the additional legend torque circa 1500 B.C.; the twenty pounds showed the ormer shell fish; the twenty five pounds bore the Royal Arms of Queen Elizabeth I with the additional legend of Royal Arms 1593 above and Elizabeth Castle below; the fifty pounds bore the arms of the Bailiwick.

diam. 23.00mm   diam. 30.00mm   diam. 36.00mm

diam. 40.01mm   common obverse

In 1977 there was a crown sized issue of a twenty five pence coin in cupro-nickel to commemorate the Silver Jubilee of Elizabeth II . The obverse had the legend Queen Elizabeth the Second 1952-1977 around the Arnold Machin bust whilst the reverse depicted Mont Orgueil Castle and Gorey harbour.

diam. 38.63mm

The issues of currency in 1981 dropped the description New from their denominations on the reverse and the date was split by the shield.

diam. 17.10mm   diam. 20.30mm   diam. 25.90mm   diam. 23.60mm

diam. 28.50mm   common obverse   diam. 30.00mm

The Royal Mint was considering introducing a pound coin as currency and asked Jersey to suggest a suitable design. As this was the bicentenary of the Battle of Jersey a commemorative square coin with rounded corners was issued. The obverse bore the legend Queen Elizabeth the Second above the Arnold Machin bust and Bailiwick of Jersey below. The reverse showed the badge of the Royal Jersey Militia with 1781 to the left and 1981 to the right surrounded by the circular legend One Pound. Bicentenary of the Battle of Jersey. It was accompanied by limited proof issues in gold and in silver which was to become the usual practise for a new coin issue.

cupro-nickel
diam. 29-70 - 25.40mm

The wedding of Prince Charles and Lady Diana Spencer was announced and the royal Mint encouraged issuing countries to strike a crown sized commemorative coin for the occasion. Various designs from different artists had been submitted and Jersey elected to use that of Michael Rizello showing the conjoined busts of the couple. The coin was struck in nickel silver, which was golden in colour, and the denomination was two pounds.

diam. 38.61mm

A new seven sided twenty pence coin was struck in 1982 to conform with a similar sized U.K. issue. On the reverse of this coin Corbière Lighthouse was illustrated with the date 1982 incuse in the rocks below.

diam. 21.40mm

New designs for Jersey coins took place in 1983. The common obverse retained a smaller Arnold Machin's crowned bust with the legend Queen Elizabeth the Second but the date of issue now appeared below. The halfpenny was discontinued. The new reverses were for the penny, Le Hocq Watch Tower; the twopence, L'Hermitage; the five pence, Seymour Tower, the ten pence, the dolmen at Faldouet; the fifty pence, Grosnez Castle. The twenty pence retained Corbiere Lighthouse and the new round pound coin bore the the first of a biannual series of the twelve Parish emblems begining with that of St Helier.

diam. 20.30mm   diam. 25.90mm   diam. 23.60mm

diam. 28.50mm   diam. 21.40mm   diam. 30.00mm   common obverse

all diam. 22.50mm

VI CONTEMPORARY COINAGE

It would seem appropriate to follow the preceding chapters by a review of Jersey coinage since decimalisation. In comparison with many other administrations there has been a conservative policy where commemorative issues are concerned. However, scrutiny of a detailed listing of the local issues indicates that the situation is complicated by numerous proofs in precious metals, and a number of high value gold and silver pieces which must be of interest only to investors and the most dedicated collectors. Moreover, some dates of the definitive series have been available only in sets.

This is not the place for a discussion on official policy on coinage; but one is left with the feeling that there is a tendency to extract revenue from collectors, apart from the basic requirement to provide currency for normal public needs.

There have been minor changes to the obverse designs, such as position of date and size of lettering. As from 1998, the Arnold Machin head was replaced by the Ian Rank Broadley head, as shown below:

The Raphael Maklouf head has been used on commemorative coins of £2 and over since 1985.

A nickelbrass Pound coin, similar in size to that in the U.K., was introduced in 1983. Its reverse design has changed frequently, illustrating the arms of the twelve parishes until 1989, then various types of old Jersey sailing ships. Exceptionally, in 1992, the reverse depicted the Jersey arms similar to the first Victorian coppers.

Silver proof. Tickler 1858

Percy Douglas 1861

Hebe 1861

Jersey Arms

Gemini 1864

Century 1866

Resolute 1877

diam. of all above. 22.50mm.

A special reverse design commemorating the 40th anniversary of the Liberation appeared on the 1985 issue of the 50 pence piece.

diam. 30.00mm

Sizes of the 50p, 10p and 5p coins were reduced in 1997, 1992 and 1990 respectively, in line with the U.K. coinage.

A bi-metallic circulation £2 coin, similar in size to the U.K. issue, first appeared in 1997, the reverse type being the shields of the twelve parishes.

diam. 28.50mm

Previous cupro-nickel £2 coins were commemoratives, as follows:

diam. 38.61mm

40th anniversary of Liberation 1985

Commonwealth Games 1986
diam. 38.61mm

World Wildlife Fund 1987
diam. 38.61mm

Visit of Queen Elizabeth II 1989
diam. 38.61mm

90th birthday of Queen Mother 1990
diam. 38.61mm

Coronation Anniversary 1993
diam. 38.61mm

50th Anniversary of Liberation 1995
diam. 38.61mm

Queen's 70th birthday 1996
diam. 38.61mm

A £5 cupro-nickel commemorative was issued in 1997 on the occasion of the Royal Golden Wedding.

diam. 38.61mm

It remains to mention the two "Millenniums" issued in 2000. The silver £5 piece has received some unfavourable comment, both regarding its rather unusual design and, in particular, the inflated price of issue.

diam. 38.61mm.

However, Jersey's first gold sovereign (see picture on front cover), released at a bullion price, had a much happier reception. The obverse has the Ian Rank Broadley bust, and the reverse has the figure of the Queen enthroned, similar to the reverse of the U.K. sovereign of 1989.

A simplified checklist of Jersey coinage since decimalisation may be helpful to collectors. It is restricted to coins issued for general circulation and available to the public at face value. Coins available in sets, proof coins, and precious metal pieces for collectors have been excluded. It must be remembered in this context that coins with dates not shown in this list exist.

UPDATE

The narrative of Modern Coinage left off at the issue of the new one pound coin being the first in a series depicting the twelve Parish Emblems. It was at this point in the compilation of text for this volume that plans were made to go to print. However there were certain matters to resolve before this could be effected and a number of years elapsed before consideration was again given to complete the work. During this period strikings of general circulation issue and collector coins sanctioned through the States of Jersey Treasury continued.

It was also during this period that the sudden and much lamented death of the author of the Modern Coinage editorial took place and therefore it was felt that in completing this history to the year ending 2008 the original text covering the period to the Parish emblem series should remain intact.

A perusal of popular current coin publications, wherein the many recent coinage issues of Jersey and the Channel Islands as a whole are only included as partial references, has led to the decision to make this publication as comprehensive as possible up to the end of 2009.

A quick reference table which covers all post-decimalisation issues intended for general circulation has been included. A cursory glance will reveal the fact that there are quite prominent gaps in years between some issues, signifying that the total number of collectable coins to form a complete collection is not in fact that great. It is envisaged that this fact alone may stimulate the reader to form a complete collection of all circulating issues. With few exceptions most can still be found in current change.

The value of a coin depends primarily on its condition and often one sees issues from twenty or so years ago with their full lustre. It should be emphasised here that on no account should a coin be cleaned, that process will immediately destroy any perceived value and render it generally unattractive.

The terminology used to describe various conditions and type of manufacture of coinage is outlined as follows:

Flan: The blank circular disc of metal upon which the coin is struck.

Proof: A coin struck from polished dies onto a polished flan giving a mirror-like finish to the coin. Although legal tender not generally intended to be so, and usually they are struck in silver or gold.

Piedfort: As above, but the flan is of a much heavier specification, generally twice the normal thickness.

Bright Uncirculated: The sheet of metal from which the coin blanks are stamped out has ben either mechanically or chemically polished, giving a lustrous appearance to the finished coin, but not to be confused with a proof. Intended primarily for the official 'Year Sets', being issued in plastic-sealed cases or presentation wallets.

Included at the end of this section are two listings in tabular form. The first shows the years of issue of Jersey circulating coinage up to 2009. The appropriate box is marked with a x.

As previously mentioned coins do exist outside of these specifically marked but the number is of such a low issue as to render the finding in circulation difficult. However they have appeared from time to time.

The second is an attempt to comprehensively list details of every Jersey coin minted since decimalisation as at the end of 2009. Most of these, with exceptions of those shown in the preceding table are struck in specimen or proof state in noble metals for the specialist collector and investor. They are however a legal tender coin for the face value they bear. All relevant information has been provided by members of the Numismatics Section of the Société Jersiaise and the States of Jersey Treasury.

Opposite: Table which covers all post-decimalisation issues intended for general circulation. Key: x = issued; so = only in set, some of which were subsequently broken up. If two columns of £1 are marked there are two different issues for that year.

YEAR	½p	1p	2p	5p	10p	20p	50p	£1	£1	£2
1968				x	x					
1969							x			
1970										
1971	x	x	x							
1972										
1973										
1974										
1975			x		x					
1976										
1977										
1978										
1979										
1980	x	x	x	x	x		x			
1981	x	x	x	x	x		x	x		
1982						x				
1983		x	x	x	x	x	x	x		
1984		x	x	x	x	x	x	x	x	
1985		x	x	x	x		x	x	x	
1986		x	x	x	x	x	x	x	x	
1987		x	x	XSO	x	x	x	x	x	
1988		x	x	x	x		x	x	x	
1989		x	x		x	x	x	x		
1990		x	x	x	x		x			
1991				x				x	x	
1992		XSO	x	XSO	x	XSO	XSO	x	x	
1993				x				x	x	
1994		x				x	x	x		
1995										
1996						x				
1997		x	XSO	XSO	XSO	x	x	x		XSO
1998		x	x	x		x	x	x		x
1999										
2000										
2001										
2002		x	x	x	x	x		x		
2003		x	x	x	x	x	x	x		x
2004										
2005		x	x	x	x	x	x	x		x
2006		x	x	x	x	x	x	x		x
2007					x	x				x
2008		x	x	x						
2009						x	x			

Glossary of abbreviations used to denote metallic composition

Cu	Copper
Cu/Steel	Copper plated Steel
Ag/Cu	Silver plated Copper
Br	Bronze
Cu-Ni	Cupro-Nickel
Ni-Ag	Nickel Silver (note-does not contain silver)
Brass/Cu-Ni	Brass outer, Cupro-Nickel inner
Ni-Brass	Nickel-Brass
Ag	Silver
Au:Ag/Ag	Gold plated Silver outer /Silver inner
Au/Ag	Gold plated Silver
Au	Gold
Pl	Platinum

EAR	F.Value	currency	JERSEY Series/ subject	Metal	Mintage	REV.	Remarks
68	5p	X	currency-1st. Decimal	Cu-Ni	3,600,000	arms + value	
	10p	X	currency-1st. Decimal	Cu-Ni	1,500,000	arms + value	
69	50p	X	currency-1st. Decimal	Cu-Ni	480,000	arms + value	
70			NO ISSUES				
71	1/2p	X	currency-1st. Decimal	Br	3,000,000	arms + value	
	1p	X	currency-1st. Decimal	Br	4,500,000	arms + value	
	2p	X	currency-1st. Decimal	Br	2,225,000	arms + value	
72	50p		Royal Wedding	Ag	23,500	Royal Mace and Map of Jersey.	.925 Ag 23mm.
	50p		Royal Wedding	Ag	1,500	Royal Mace and Map of Jersey.	PROOF .925 Ag 23mm.
	£1		Royal Wedding	Ag	23,500	Jersey Lily	.925 Ag 30 mm.
	£1		Royal Wedding	Ag	1,500	Jersey Lily	PROOF .925 Ag 30mm.
	£2		Royal Wedding	Ag	23,500	The Barque "Alexandra"	.925 Ag 36 mm.
	£2		Royal Wedding	Ag	1,500	The Barque "Alexandra"	PROOF .925 Ag 36 mm.
	£2-50		Royal Wedding	Ag	23,500	Lobster	.925 Ag 40 mm.
	£2-50		Royal Wedding	Ag	1,500	Lobster	PROOF .925 Ag 40 mm.
	£5		Royal Wedding	Au	8,500	Lesser White-toothed Shrew	.916 Au 14.5 mm.
	£5		Royal Wedding	Au	1500	Lesser White-toothed Shrew	PROOF .916 Au 14.5 mm.
	£10		Royal Wedding	Au	8,500	Bronze Age Gold Torque	.916 Au 18 mm.
	£10		Royal Wedding	Au	1500	Bronze Age Gold Torque	PROOF .916 Au 18 mm.
	£20		Royal Wedding	Au	8,500	The Ormer (Haliotis tuberculata)	.916 Au 22.5 mm.
	£20		Royal Wedding	Au	1500	The Ormer (Haliotis tuberculata)	PROOF 916 Au 22.5 mm.
	£25		Royal Wedding	Au	8,500	Arms of Q.E. 1st.	.916 Au 25 mm.
	£25		Royal Wedding	Au	1500	Arms of Q.E. 1st.	PROOF .916 Au 25 mm.
	£50		Royal Wedding	Au	8,500	Arms of Bailiwick	.916 Au 31 mm.
	£50		Royal Wedding	Au	1500	Arms of Bailiwick (set number on edge)	PROOF .916 Au 31 mm.
73			NO ISSUES				
74			NO ISSUES				
75	2p	X	currency	Br	750,000	arms+value	
	10p	X	currency	Cu-Ni	1,022,000	arms+value	
76			NO ISSUES				
77	25p		Silver Jubilee	Cu-Ni	255,510	Gorey Castle	
	25p		Silver Jubilee	Ag	35,000	Gorey Castle	PROOF .925 Ag
78			NO ISSUES				
79	10p	X	currency	Cu-Ni		arms+value dated 1975 thicker flan	
80	1/2p	X	currency	Br	200,000	arms+value	
	1/2p		proof	Br	10,000	arms+value	contained in set.
	1p	X	currency	Br	3,000,000	arms+value	
	1p		proof	Br	10,000	arms+value	contained in set
	2p	X	currency	Br	2,000,000	arms+value	
	2p		proof	Br	10,000	arms+value	contained in set
	5p	X	currency	Cu-Ni	800,000	arms+value	
	5p		proof	Cu-Ni	10,000	arms+value	contained in set.
	10p	X	currency	Cu-Ni	1,000,000	arms+value	
	10p		proof	Cu-Ni	10,000	arms+value	contained in set
	50p	X	currency	Cu-Ni	100,000	arms+value	
	50p		proof	Cu-Ni	10,000	arms+value	contained in set
			PROOF SET		10,000		1/2p to 50p (see above)
81	1/2p	X	currency	Br	50,000	arms+value	
	1/2p		proof	Br	15,000	arms+value	contained in set.

Year	Denom	X	Type	Metal	Quantity	Design	Notes
	1p	X	currency	Br	50,000	arms+value	
	1p		proof	Br	15,000	arms+value	contained in set.
	2p	X	currency	Br	50,000	arms+value	
	2p		proof	Br	15,000	arms+value	contained in set.
	5p	X	currency	Cu-Ni	50,000	arms+value	
	5p		proof	Cu-Ni	15,000	arms+value	contained in set.
	10p	X	currency	Cu-Ni	50,000	arms+value	
	10p		proof	Cu-Ni	15,000	arms+value	contained in set.
	50p	X	currency	Cu-Ni	50,000	arms+value	
	50p		proof	Cu-Ni	15,000	arms+value	contained in set.
	£1	X	currency	Cu-Ni	200,000	crown+shield arms	Bi-Centenary Battle of Jsy. square form
	£1		currency	Cu-Ni	inc. above	crown+shield arms	ditto- set in card in red polythene walle
	£1		proof	Cu-Ni	15,000	crown+shield arms	contained in set.
	£1		proof	Ag	10,000	crown+shield arms	PROOF .925 Ag
	£1		proof	Au	5,000	crown+shield arms	PROOF .916 Au 15.98 gms. 28.4 m
	£2		Royal Wedding	Ni-Ag	150,000	Charles +Diana	unc.
	£2		Royal Wedding	Ni-Ag	inc.above	Charles +Diana	In red acrylic, given to all schoolchildre
	£2		Royal Wedding	Ag	35,000	Charles +Diana	PROOF .925 Ag
	£2		Royal Wedding	Au	1,500	Charles +Diana	PROOF .916 Au
			PROOF SET		15,000		1/2p to £1 (see above)
1982	20p	X	currency	Cu-Ni	200,000	Corbiere Lighthouse	
	20p		proof	Ag	1,500	Corbiere Lighthouse	PROOF Piedfort .925 Ag
1983	1p	X	currency	Br	500,000	Le Hocq	
	1p		bright uncirculated	Br	inc.above	Le Hocq	contained in sets
	1p		proof	Ag	5,000	Le Hocq	PROOF .925 Ag
	2p	X	currency	Br	800,000	Dolmen	
	2p		bright uncirculated	Br	inc. above	Dolmen	contained in sets
	2p		proof	Ag	5,000	Dolmen	PROOF .925 Ag
	5p	X	currency	Cu-Ni	400,000	Seymour Tower	
	5p		bright uncirculated	Cu-Ni	inc. above	Seymour Tower	contained in sets
	5p		proof	Ag	5,000	Seymour Tower	PROOF .925 Ag
	10p	X	currency	Cu-Ni	30,000	L'Hermitage	
	10p		bright uncirculated	Cu-Ni	inc. above	L'Hermitage	contained in sets
	10p		proof	Ag	5,000	L'Hermitage	PROOF .925 Ag
	20p	X	currency	Cu-Ni	400,000	Corbiere Lighthouse	
	20p		bright uncirculated	Cu-Ni	inc. above	Corbiere Lighthouse	contained in sets
	20p		proof	Ag	5,000	Corbiere Lighthouse	PROOF .925 Ag
	50p	X	currency	Cu-Ni	50,000	Grosnez castle	
	50p		bright uncirculated	Cu-Ni	inc. above	Grosnez castle	contained in sets
	50p		proof	Ag	5,000	Grosnez castle	PROOF .925 Ag
	£1	X	currency Parish Emblems	Ni-Brass	100,000	St. Helier	
	£1		Parish Emblems	Ni-Brass	inc. above	St. Helier	laminated in photograph of Royal Squa
	£1		Parish Emblems	Ag	10,000	St. Helier	PROOF .925 Ag
	£1		Parish Emblems	Au	1,500	St. Helier	PROOF .916 Au (467 melted down
	£1 to 1p		Presentation Set		inc.above		fold out wallet with aerial view on cove
	£1 to 1p		Proof Set	Ag	5,000		coins in acrylic capsules in red folder
1984	1p	X	currency	Br	1,000,000	Le Hocq	
	2p	X	currency	Br	750,000	Dolmen	
	5p	X	currency	Cu-Ni	300,000	Seymour tower	
	10p	X	currency	Cu-Ni	100,000	L'Hermitage	
	20p	X	currency	Cu-Ni	250,000	Corbiere	
	50p	X	currency	Cu-Ni	50,000	Grosnez Castle	
	£1	X	currency Parish Emblems	Ni-Brass	20,000	St. Saviour	
	£1		Parish Emblems	Ni-Brass	inc. above	St.Saviour	presentation -red wallet
	£1		Parish Emblems	Ag	2,500	St. Saviour	PROOF .925 Ag
	£1		Parish Emblems	Au	250	St. Saviour	PROOF .916 Au
	£1	X	currency Parish Emblems	Ni-Brass	20,000	St. Brelade	

	£1		Parish Emblems	Ni-Brass	inc. above	St. Brelade	presentation -red wallet
	£1		Parish Emblems	Ag	2,500	St. Brelade	PROOF .925 Ag
	£1		Parish Emblems	Au	250	St. Brelade	PROOF .916 Au
85	1p	X	currency	Br	1,000,000	Le Hocq	
	2p	X	currency	Br	250,000	Dolmen	
	5p	X	currency	Cu-Ni	600,000	Seymour Tower	
	10p	X	currency	Cu-Ni	100,000	L'Hermitage	
	50p	X	currency, 40th. Liberation	Cu-Ni	65,000	crossed flags +chain	
	£1	X	currency Parish Emblems	Ni-Brass	25,000	St. Clement	
	£1		Parish Emblems	Ni-Brass	inc.above	St. Clement	presentation -red wallet
	£1		Parish Emblems	Ag	2,500	St. Clement	PROOF .925 Ag
	£1		Parish Emblems	Au	250	St. Clement	PROOF .916 Au
	£1	X	currency Parish Emblems	Ni-Brass	10,000	St. Lawrence	
	£1		Parish Emblems	Ni-Brass	inc.above	St. Lawrence	presentation -red wallet
	£1		Parish Emblems	Ag	2,500	St. Lawrence	PROOF .925 Ag
	£1		Parish Emblems	Au	250	St. Lawrence	PROOF .916 Au
	£2		Liberation 40th. Anniversary	Cu-Ni	5,000	H.M.S.Beagle	edge inscrip "today our etc"
	£2		Liberation 40th. Anniversary	Cu-Ni	15,000	H.M.S.Beagle	Plastic cased given to all Schoolchildren
	£2		Liberation 40th. Anniversary	Ag	2,500	H.M.S.Beagle	Proof edge inscrip "today our etc" .925Ag
	£2		Liberation 40th. Anniversary	Au	40	H.M.S.Beagle	Proof edge inscrip "today our etc" .916 Au
86	1p	X	currency	Br	2,000,000	Le Hocq	
	2p	X	currency	Br	1,000,000	Dolmen	
	5p	X	currency	Cu-Ni	200,000	Seymour Tower	
	10p	X	currency	Cu-Ni	400,000	L'Hermitage	
	20p	X	currency	Cu-Ni	100,000	Corbiere Lighthouse	
	50p	X	currency	Cu-Ni	30,000	Grosnez Castle	
	£1	X	currency Parish Emblems	Ni-Brass	10,000	St. Peter	
	£1		Parish Emblems	Ni-Brass	inc. above	St. Peter	presentation -red wallet
	£1		Parish Emblems	Ag	2,500	St. Peter	PROOF .925 Ag
	£1		Parish Emblems	Au	250	St. Peter	PROOF .916 Au
	£1	X	currency Parish Emblems	Ni-Brass	10,000	Grouville	
	£1		Parish Emblems	Ni-Brass	inc. above	Grouville	presentation -red wallet
	£1		Parish Emblems	Ag	2,500	Grouville	PROOF .925 Ag
	£1		Parish Emblems	Au	250	Grouville	PROOF .916 Au
	£2	commem.	Commonwealth Games	Cu-Ni	50,000	two runners	edge inscr."XIII Commonwealth Games"
	£2	commem.	Commonwealth Games	Cu-Ni	5,000	two runners	Presentation case- no edge inscription
	£2	commem.	Commonwealth Games	Ag	50,000	two runners	PROOF .500 Ag
	£2	commem.	Commonwealth Games	Ag	20,000	two runners	PROOF .925 Ag
87	1p	X	currency	Br	1,500,000	Le Hocq	
	1p		bright uncirculated specimen	Br	5,500	Le Hocq	contained in specimen set
	2p	X	currency	Br	2,000,000	Dolmen	
	2p		bright uncirculated specimen	Br	5,500	Dolmen	contained in specimen set
	5p		bright uncirculated specimen	Cu-Ni	5,500	Seymour Tower	contained in specimen set
	10p	X	currency	Cu-Ni	800,000	L'Hermitage	
	10p		bright uncirculated specimen	Cu-Ni	5,500	L'Hermitage	contained in specimen set
	20p	X	currency	Cu-Ni	100,000	Corbiere Lighthouse	
	20p		bright uncirculated specimen	Cu-Ni	5,500	Corbiere Lighthouse	contained in specimen set
	50p	X	currency	Cu-Ni	150,000	Grosnez castle	
	50p		bright uncirculated specimen	Cu-Ni	5,500	Grosnez castle	contained in specimen set
	£1	X	currency Parish Emblems	Ni-Brass	10,000	St. Martin	
	£1		Parish Emblems	Ni-Brass	inc. above	St. Martin	presentation -red wallet
	£1		Parish Emblems specimen	Ni-Brass	5,500	St. Martin	contained in specimen set
	£1		Parish Emblems	Ag	2,500	St. Martin	PROOF .925 Ag
	£1		Parish Emblems	Au	250	St. Martin	PROOF .916 Au
	£1	X	currency Parish Emblems	Ni-Brass	10,000	St. Ouen	
	£1		Parish Emblems	Ni-Brass	inc. above	St. Ouen	presentation -red wallet
	£1		Parish Emblems	Ag	2,500	St. Ouen	PROOF .925 Ag

Year	Denom	X	Description	Metal	Mintage	Design	Notes
	£1		Parish Emblems	Au	250	St. Ouen	PROOF .916 Au
	£2		W.W.F. 25th. Anniversary	Cu-Ni	22,500	MauritiusPink Pigeon	unc.
	£2		W.W.F. 25th. Anniversary	Cu-Ni	inc.above	MauritiusPink Pigeon	presentation blister pack
	£2		W.W.F. 25th. Anniversary	Ag	25,000	MauritiusPink Pigeon	PROOF .925 Ag
	£1 to 1p		Specimen set		5,500		slip case with Parish emblems on cover
1988	1p	X	currency	Br	1,000,000	Le Hocq	
	2p	X	currency	Br	750,000	Dolmen	
	5p	X	currency	Cu-Ni	400,000	Seymour Tower	
	10p	X	currency	Cu-Ni	650,000	L'Hermitage	
	50p	X	currency	Cu-Ni	130,000	Grosnez Castle	
	£1	X	currency Parish Emblems	Ni-Brass	10,000	Trinity	
	£1		Parish Emblems	Ni-Brass	inc. above	Trinity	presentation -red wallet
	£1		Parish Emblems	Ag	2,500	Trinity	PROOF .925 Ag
	£1		Parish Emblems	Au	250	Trinity	PROOF .916 Au
	£1	X	currency Parish Emblems	Ni-Brass	10,000	St. John	
	£1		Parish Emblems	Ni-Brass	inc. above	St. John	presentation -red wallet
	£1		Parish Emblems	Ag	2,500	St. John	PROOF .925 Ag
	£1		Parish Emblems	Au	250	St. John	PROOF .916 Au
1989	1p	X	currency	Br	1,500,000	Le Hocq	
	2p	X	currency	Br	1,000,000	Dolmen	
	10p	X	currency	Cu-Ni	700,000	L'Hermitage	
	20p	X	currency	Cu-Ni	100,000	Corbiere Lighthouse	
	50p	X	currency	Cu-Ni	180,000	Grosnez Castle	
	£1	X	currency Parish Emblems	Ni-Brass	25,000	St. Mary	
	£1		Parish Emblems	Ni-Brass	inc. above	St. Mary	presentation red wallet
	£1		Parish Emblems	Ag	2,500	St. Mary	PROOF .925 Ag
	£1		Parish Emblems	Au	250	St. Mary	PROOF .916 Au
	£2		Royal Visit	Cu-Ni	10,000	Island Map + Mace	edge legend faces obv.
	£2		Royal Visit	Cu-Ni	inc. above	Island Map + Mace	edge legend faces rev.
	£2		Royal Visit	Ag	3,000	Island Map + Mace	PROOF .925 Ag
1990	1p	X	currency	Br	2,000,000	Le Hocq	
	2p	X	currency	Br	3,000,000	Dolmen	
	5p	X	currency	Cu-Ni	4,000,000	Seymour Tower	
	10p	X	currency	Cu-Ni	850,000	L'Hermitage	
	50p	X	currency	Cu-Ni	370,000	Grosnez Castle	
	£2		Queen Mother 90th. B/Day.	Cu-Ni	10,000	Crowned Cypher + dates.	
	£2		Queen Mother 90th. B/Day.	Ag	3,000	Crowned Cypher + dates.	PROOF .925 Ag
	£2		Queen Mother 90th. B/Day.	Au	90	Crowned Cypher + dates.	PROOF .916 Au
	£2		50th. Anniv. Battle of Britain	Ag	10,000	Spitfire over S.England	PROOF .925 Ag
	£5		50th. Anniv. Battle of Britain	Ag	5,000	Spitfire over S.England	PROOF .925Ag 65mm. 5 ozs. 155.6gms
	£10		50th. Anniv. Battle of Britain	Au	500	Crowned Air Force Badge	PROOF .999 Au
	£25		50th. Anniv. Battle of Britain	Au	500	Spitfire over S.England	PROOF .999 Au
	£50		50th. Anniv. Battle of Britain	Au	500	Crowned Air Force Badge	PROOF .999 Au
	£100		50th. Anniv. Battle of Britain	Au	500	Spitfire over S.England	PROOF .999 Au
1991	5p	X	currency	Cu-Ni	2,000,000	Seymour Tower	
	£1	X	currency Ship series.	Ni-Brass	15,000	"The Tickler"	
	£1		Ship series	Ni-Brass	inc.above	"The Tickler"	Presentation card.
	£1		Ship series	Ag	3,000	"The Tickler"	PROOF .925 Ag
	£1		Ship series	Au	250	"The Tickler"	PROOF Piedfort .916 Au 19.5 gms
	£1	X	currency Ship series.	Ni-Brass	20,000	"Percy Douglas"	
	£1		Ship series	Ni-Brass	inc.above	"Percy Douglas"	Presentation card.
	£1		Ship series	Ag	3,000	"Percy Douglas"	PROOF .925 Ag
	£1		Ship series	Au	250	"Percy Douglas"	PROOF Piedfort .916 Au 19.5 gms
1992	1p		bright uncirculated specimen	Br	6,000	Le Hocq	only issued in year set
	2p	X	currency	Cu/Steel	2,250,000	Dolmen	

	2p		bright uncirculated specimen Br		6,000	Dolmen	issued in year set
	5p		bright uncirculated specimen Cu-Ni		6,000	Seymour Tower	only issued in year set
	10p	X	currency	Cu-Ni	700,000	L'Hermitage	
	10p		bright uncirculated specimen Cu-Ni		6,000	L'Hermitage	issued in year set
	20p		bright uncirculated specimen Cu-Ni		6,000	La Corbiere	only issued in year set
	50p		bright uncirculated specimen Cu-Ni		6,000	Grosnez Castle	issued in year set
	£1	X	currency Ship series.	Ni-Brass	20,000	"Hebe"	
	£1		bright uncirculated specimen Ni-Brass		inc. above	"Hebe"	issued in year set.
	£1		Ship series	Ni-Brass	inc.above	"Hebe"	Presentation card.
	£1		Ship series	Ag	3,000	"Hebe"	PROOF .925 Ag
	£1		Ship series	Au	250	"Hebe"	PROOF Piedfort .916 Au 19.5 gms.
	£1	X	currency Ship series.	Ni-Brass	20,000	"Coat of Arms"	
	£1		Ship series	Ni-Brass	inc.above	"Coat of Arms"	Presentation card.
	£1		Ship series	Ag	3,000	"Coat of Arms"	PROOF
	£1		Ship series	Au	250	"Coat of Arms"	PROOF Piedfort .916 Au 19.5 gms.
	£1 to 1p		presentation set		6000 sets		In descriptive folder
993	5p	X	currency	Cu-Ni	2,000,000	Seymour Tower	
	£1	X	currency Ship series.	Ni-Brass	20,000	"Gemini"	
	£1		Ship series	Ni-Brass	inc.above	"Gemini"	Presentation card.
	£1		Ship series	Ag	3,000	"Gemini"	PROOF .925 Ag
	£1		Ship series	Au	250	"Gemini"	PROOF Piedfort .916 Au 19.5 gms.
	£1	X	currency Ship series.	Ni-Brass	20,000	"Century"	
	£1		Ship series	Ni-Brass	inc.above	"Century"	Presentation card.
	£1		Ship series	Ag	3,000	"Century"	PROOF .925 Ag
	£1		Ship series	Au	250	"Century"	PROOF Piedfort .916 Au 19.5 gms.
	£2		40th. Anniv. Coronation	Cu-Ni	12,000	Crown+Mace	
	£2		40th. Anniv. Coronation	Ag	10,000	Crown+Mace	PROOF .925 Ag
	£2		40th. Anniv. Coronation	Au	40	Crown+Mace	PROOF .916 Au
994	1p	X	currency	Cu/Steel	2,000,000	Le Hocq	
	20p	X	currency	Cu-Ni	200,000	Corbiere Lighthouse	
	50p	X	currency	Cu-Ni	200,000	Grosnez Castle	30 mm.
	£1	X	currency Ship series.	Ni-Brass	60,000	"Resolute"	
	£1		Ship series	Ni-Brass	inc.above	"Resolute"	Presentation card.
	£1		Ship series	Ag	3,000	"Resolute"	PROOF .925 Ag
	£1		Ship series	Au	250	"Resolute"	PROOF Piedfort .916 Au 19.5 gms.
995			NO CURRENCY ISSUES				
	£2		50th. Anniv. Of Liberation	Cu-Ni	42,000	Dove+Victory Sign	
	£2		50th. Anniv. Of Liberation	Cu-Ni	inc.above	Dove+Victory Sign	selected contained in a plastic case
	£2		50th. Anniv. Of Liberation	Ag	7,000	Dove+Victory Sign	PROOF .925 Ag
	£2		50th. Anniv. Of Liberation	Ag		Dove+Victory Sign	PROOF- PIEDFORT .925 Ag
	£10		50th. Anniv. Of Liberation	Au	500	Red Cross ship Vega	PROOF .999 Au 3.13 gms.
	£25		50th. Anniv. Of Liberation	Au	500	Family and Flags	PROOF .999 Au 7.81 gms.
	£50		50th. Anniv. Of Liberation	Au	500	Victory sign,soldiers and flags	PROOF .999 Au 15.61gms.
	£100		50th. Anniv. Of Liberation	Au	500	Map of Island with Dove and Shield.	PROOF .999 Au 31.21gms.
996	20p	X	currency	Cu-Ni	250,000	Corbiere Lighthouse	
	£2		Q.E. II 70th. Birthday	Cu-Ni	4,000	Floret of Lilies	
	£2		Q.E. II 70th. Birthday	Cu-Ni	inc. above	Floret of Lilies	unc. Encapsulated in Presentation Card.
	£2		Q.E. II 70th. Birthday	Ag	12,500	Floret of Lilies	PROOF .925 Ag
997	1p	X	currency	Cu/Steel	320,000	Le Hocq	
	1p			Cu/Steel	5,500	Le Hocq	B.U. In sets.
	2p			Cu/Steel	5,500	Dolmen	B.U. In sets only.
	5p			Cu-Ni	5,500	Seymour Tower	B.U. In sets only.
	10p			Cu-Ni	5,500	L'Hermitage	B.U. In sets only.
	20p	X	currency	Cu-Ni	600,000	Corbiere Lighthouse	
	20p			Cu-Ni	5,500	Corbiere Lighthouse	B.U. In sets only

	50p	X	currency	Cu-Ni	1,500,000	Grosnez Castle	27.3 mm.
	50p			Cu-Ni	5,500	Grosnez Castle	B.U. In sets. 27.3 mm.
	50p			Cu-Ni	5,500	Grosnez Castle	B.U. In sets. 30 mm.
	£1	X	currency Ship series	Ni-Brass	101,000	"Resolute"	
	£1			Ni-Brass	5,500	"Resolute" B.U. In sets.	
	£2			NiBr/ Cu-Ni	5,500	Parish Emblems	B.U. In sets only. Ni-Br out /Cu-Ni inne
	£2			Au:Ag / Ag	500	Parish Emblems	PROOF Au on Ag outer, Ag inner.
	£5		Royal Golden Wedding	Cu-Ni	6,000	H.M.Queen+Philip	
	£5		Royal Golden Wedding	Ag	30,000	H.M.Queen+Philip, gold cameo shield	PROOF .925 Ag
	£2 to 1p		Specimen set		5,500		most sets broken up and coins circulated
1998	1p	X	currency	Cu/Steel	6,350,000	Le Hocq	
	2p	X	currency	Cu/Steel	3,750,000	Dolmen	
	5p	X	currency	Cu-Ni	3,200,000	Seymour Tower	
	20p	X	currency	Cu-Ni	900,000	Corbiere Lighthouse	
	50p	X	currency	Cu-Ni	2,000,000	Grosnez Castle	27.3 mm.
	£1	X	currency	Ni-Brass	374,000	"Resolute"	
	£2	X	currency	NiBr/ Cu-Ni	720,000	Parish Emblems	Outer ring,Nickel- Brass / Inner circle Cu-N
1999			NO ISSUES				
2000	£5		Millenium	Ag	32,000	Globe + Island gold highlighted	PROOF .925 Ag
	Sovereign		Millenium Commemorative	Au	2,000	King William seated on Throne	.916 Au
	Sovereign		Millenium Commemorative	Au	2,000	King William seated on Throne	PROOF .916 Au
2001			NO ISSUES				
2002	1p	X	currency	Cu/Steel	1,520,000	Le Hocq	
	2p	X	currency	Cu/Steel	1,259,000	Dolmen	
	5p	X	currency	Cu-Ni	1,200,000	Seymour tower	
	10p	X	currency	Cu-Ni	500,000	L'Hermitage	
	20p	X	currency	Cu-Ni	975,500	Corbiere	
	£1	X	currency	Ni-Brass	335,000	"Resolute"	
	£5		Diana Memorial	Cu-Ni		Cameo portrait above Children	part of p/pack inc.Guer. + Ald.
	£5		Diana Memorial	Ag	20,000	Cameo portrait above Children	PROOF .925 Ag
	£5		Diana Memorial	Au	100	Cameo portrait above Children	PROOF .916 Au 22mm.
	£25		Diana Memorial	Au	2,500	Cameo with a flower + wreath.	PROOF .916Au 7.98gms 22.05mm
	£5		Queen Mother commem.	Cu-Ni		Young Queen Mother portrait	
	£5		Queen Mother commem.	Ag	15,000	Young Queen Mother portrait	PROOF .925 Ag
	£5		Queen Mother commem.	Au	250	Young Queen Mother portrait	PROOF .916 Au 39.94 gms. 38.6mm
	£25		Queen Mother commem.	Au	2,500	Young Queen Mother portrait	PROOF .916 Au 7.98 gms. 22 mm
	£5		Golden Jubilee	Cu-Ni		Abbey procession scene	
	£5		Golden Jubilee	Ag	20,000	Abbey procession scene (Au Cameo)	PROOF .925 Ag
	£5		Golden Jubilee	Au	100	Abbey procession scene	PROOF .916 Au 39.94 gms. 38.6mm
	£5		Golden Jubilee	Au	100	Abbey procession scene	PROOF Piedfort .916 Au 56.56gms
	£25		Golden Jubilee	Au	2,500	Abbey procession scene	PROOF .916 Au 7.98 gms. 22 mm
	£5		Duke of Wellington	Cu-Ni		Portrait + infantry scene coloured highlights on rev.	
	£5		Duke of Wellington	Ag	15,000	Portrait + infantry scene	PROOF .925 Ag
	£5		Duke of Wellington	Au	200	Portrait + infantry scene	PROOF .916 Au 39.94 gms. 38.6mm
	£25		Duke of Wellington	Au	2,500	Portrait + infantry scene	PROOF .916 Au 22 mm.
2003	1p	X	currency	Cu/Steel	1,575,000	Le Hocq	
	2p	X	currency	Cu/Steel	10,000	Dolmen	
	5p	X	currency	Cu-Ni	1,005,000	Seymour Tower	
	10p	X	currency	Cu-Ni	10,000	L'Hermitage	
	20p	X	currency	Cu-Ni	10,000	Corbiere	
	50p	X	currency	Cu-Ni	10,000	Grosnez Castle	
	50p	X	currency	Cu-Ni		Crowning ceremony	
	50p		Golden Coronation Anniv.	Ag	15,000	Crowning ceremony	PROOF .925 Ag
	50p	X	currency	Cu-Ni		Crown,Orb + Sceptres	

50p		Golden Coronation Anniv.	Ag	15,000	Crown, Orb + Sceptres	PROOF .925 Ag
50p	X	currency	Cu-Ni		Queen on Throne	
50p		Golden Coronation Anniv.	Ag	15,000	Queen on Throne	PROOF .925 Ag
50p	X	currency	Cu-Ni		Crown, Mace and Arms	
50p		Golden Coronation Anniv.	Ag	15,000	Crown, Mace and Arms PROOF	.925 Ag
£10		Golden Coronation Anniv.	Au / Ag	2,000	Crown, Mace and Arms. PROOF	65mm. 5 ozs. .925 Ag
£1	X	currency	Ni-Brass	10,000	"Resolute"	
£2	X	currency	NiBr/ Cu-Ni	10,000	Parish Emblems	outer Nickel- Brass /Inner circle Cu-Ni
£5		Golden Jubilee	Cu-Ni		Honour Guard + Cenotaph	Polished die
£5		Golden Jubilee	Ag	20,000	Honour Guard + Cenotaph	PROOF .925 Ag
£5		Golden Jubilee	Au	250	Honour Guard + Cenotaph	PROOF .916 Au 39.94 gms. 38.6mm
£25		Golden Jubilee	Au	5,000	Honour Guard + Cenotaph	PROOF .916 Au 7.98 gms 22mm
£50		Golden Jubilee	Ag	500	Facing bust + crowned arms	PROOF 1 Kg. .925 Ag 100 mm.
£5		Prince William 21st. B/day.	Cu-Ni		Prince William in Jacket +Tie	
£5		Prince William 21st. B/day.	Ag	10,000	Prince William in Jacket +Tie	PROOF .925 Ag
£5		Prince William 21st. B/day.	Au	200	Prince William in Jacket +Tie	PROOF .916 Au 39.94 gms. 38.6mm
£5		History of the Royal Navy	Cu-Ni		Naval Commanders	flag highlight
£5		History of the Royal Navy	Cu-Ni		Naval Commanders	PROOF flag highlight
£5		History of the Royal Navy	Ag		Naval Commanders	PROOF flag highlight .925 Ag
£5		History of the Royal Navy	Au	low	Naval Commanders	PROOF .916 Au 39.94 gms. 38.6mm
£25		History of the Royal Navy	Au		Naval Commanders	PROOF .916 Au 22 mm.
£5		History of the Royal Navy	Cu-Ni		Francis Drake	
£5		History of the Royal Navy	Ag		Francis Drake	PROOF flag highlight .925 Ag
£5		History of the Royal Navy	Au	low	Francis Drake	PROOF .916 Au 39.94 gms. 38.6mm
£25		History of the Royal Navy	Au		Francis Drake	PROOF .916 Au 7.98gms. 22mm
£5		History of the Royal Navy	Cu-Ni		Sovereign of the Seas.	
£5		History of the Royal Navy	Ag		Sovereign of the Seas.	PROOF flag highlight .925 Ag
£5		History of the Royal Navy	Au	low	Sovereign of the Seas.	PROOF .916 Au 39.94 gms. 38.6mm
£25		History of the Royal Navy	Au		Sovereign of the Seas.	PROOF .916 Au 7.98. gms. 22mm.

004

NO CURRENCY ISSUES

£5		60th. Anniv. "D" Day	Cu-Ni		Horsa Gliders + Parachutists	
£5		60th. Anniv. "D" Day	Ag	25,000	Horsa Gliders + Parachutists	PROOF red poppy highlight .925 Ag
£5		60th. Anniv. "D" Day	Au	500	Horsa Gliders + Parachutists	PROOF .916 Au 38.6mm.
£25		60th. Anniv. "D" Day	Au	500	Horsa Gliders + Parachutists	PROOF .916 Au 7.98gms 22 mm.
£5		Crimea	Cu-Ni		Charge of Light Brigade	blue uniform highlight
£5		Crimea	Ag	10,000	Charge of Light Brigade	PROOF blue uniform highlight .925Ag
£5		Crimea	Au	500	Charge of Light Brigade	PROOF .916 Au 39.94 gms. 38.6mm
£10		Crimea	Ag	1,854	Charge of Light Brigade	PROOF 65mm. 925 Ag
£25		Crimea	Au		Charge of Light Brigade	PROOF .916 Au 7.98gms. 22mm.
£5		History of the Royal Navy	Cu-Ni		H.M.S. Victory	unc.
£5		History of the Royal Navy	Ag		H.M.S. Victory	PROOF flag highlight .925 Ag.
£5		History of the Royal Navy	Au	low	H.M.S. Victory	PROOF .916 Au 39.94 gms. 38.6mm
£25		History of the Royal Navy	Au		H.M.S. Victory	PROOF .916 Au 7.98gms. 22mm.
£5		History of the Royal Navy	Cu-Ni		John Fisher 1841 - 1920	unc.
£5		History of the Royal Navy	Ag		John Fisher 1841 - 1920	PROOF flag highlight .925 Ag.
£5		History of the Royal Navy	Au	low	John Fisher 1841 - 1920	PROOF .916 Au 39.94 gms. 38.6mm
£25		History of the Royal Navy	Au		John Fisher 1841 - 1920	PROOF .916 Au 7.98gms. 22mm.
£5		Golden age of Steam	Cu-Ni		The Coronation Scot.	
£5		Golden age of Steam	Ag	15,000	The Coronation Scot.	PROOF .925 Ag
£5		Golden age of Steam	Au	low	The Coronation Scot.	PROOF .916 Au 39.94 gms. 38.6mm
£25		Golden age of Steam	Au		The Coronation Scot.	PROOF .916 Au 7.98gms. 22mm.
£5		Golden age of Steam	Cu-Ni	22,000	Flying Scotsman	
£5		Golden age of Steam	Ag		Flying Scotsman	PROOF .925 Ag.
£5		Golden age of Steam	Au / Ag		Flying Scotsman	PROOF .925 Ag gilt
£5		Golden age of Steam	Au	low	Flying Scotsman	PROOF .916 Au 39.94 gms. 38.6mm
£25		Golden age of Steam	Au		Flying Scotsman	PROOF .916 Au 7.98gms. 22mm.
£5		Golden age of Steam	Cu-Ni		Golden Arrow	
£5		Golden age of Steam	Ag		Golden Arrow	PROOF .925 Ag.
£5		Golden age of Steam	Au	low	Golden Arrow	PROOF .916 Au 39.94 gms. 38.6mm

	£25		Golden age of Steam	Au		Golden Arrow	PROOF .916 Au 7.98gms. 22mm
	£5		Golden age of Steam	Cu-Ni		Driver and Fireman	
	£5		Golden age of Steam	Ag		Driver and Fireman	PROOF .925 Ag.
	£5		Golden age of Steam	Au	low	Driver and Fireman	PROOF .916 Au 39.94 gms. 38.6m
	£5		Golden age of Steam	Cu-Ni		Box Tunnel and King Loco.	
	£5		Golden age of Steam	Ag		Box Tunnel and King Loco.	PROOF .925 Ag.
	£5		Golden age of Steam	Au	low	Box Tunnel and King Loco.	PROOF .916 Au 39.94 gms. 38.6m
	£5		Golden age of Steam	Cu-Ni		Rocket and Evening Star	
	£5		Golden age of Steam	Ag		Rocket and Evening Star	PROOF .925 Ag
	£5		Golden age of Steam	Au / Ag		Rocket and Evening Star	PROOF .925 Ag
	£5		Golden age of Steam	Au	low	Rocket and Evening Star	PROOF .916 Au 39.94 gms. 38.6m
	£25		Golden age of Steam	Au		Rocket and Evening Star	PROOF .916 Au 7.98gms. 22mm
2005	1p	X	currency	Cu/Steel		Le Hocq	not officially listed but seen in circulatio
	2p	X	currency	Cu/Steel	400,000	Dolmen	
	5p	X	currency	Cu-Ni	very low	Seymour Tower	
	10p	X	currency	Cu-Ni	very low	L'Hermitage	
	20p	X	currency	Cu-Ni	500,000	Corbiere Lighthouse	
	50p	X	currency	Cu-Ni	200,000	Grosnez Castle	
	£1	X	currency	Ni-Brass	low	"Resolute"	
	£2	X	currency	NiBr/ Cu-Ni	very low	Parish Emblems	outer Nickel- Brass /Inner circle Cu-l
	£5		History of the Royal Navy	Cu-Ni		Andrew Cunningham	unc.
	£5		History of the Royal Navy	Ag		Andrew Cunningham	PROOF .925 Ag
	£5		History of the Royal Navy	Au	50	Andrew Cunningham	PROOF .916 Au 39.94 gms. 38.6m
	£25		History of the Royal Navy	Au		Andrew Cunningham	PROOF 19 mm. .916 Au
	£5		History of the Royal Navy	Cu-Ni		H.M.S. Conqueror	unc.
	£5		History of the Royal Navy	Ag		H.M.S. Conqueror	PROOF .925 Ag
	£5		History of the Royal Navy	Au	50	H.M.S. Conqueror	PROOF .916 Au 39.94 gms. 38.6m
	£25		History of the Royal Navy	Au		H.M.S. Conqueror	PROOF .916 Au 7.98gms. 22mm
	£5		Battle of Trafalgar	Cu-Ni		200th. Anniversary Nelson.	unc.
	£5		Battle of Trafalgar	Ag		200th. Anniv. Nelson. Au h/light ship	PROOF .925 Ag
	£5		Battle of Trafalgar	Au		200th. Anniversary Nelson.	PROOF .916 Au 9 mm. 1.244gms
	£5		Battle of Trafalgar	Au	low	200th. Anniversary Nelson.	PROOF .916 Au 39.94 gms. 38.6m
	£10		Battle of Trafalgar	Ag		200th. Anniversary Nelson.	PROOF 65mm. 5ozs. 925 Ag
	£10		Battle of Trafalgar	Au / Ag		200th. Anniversary Nelson.	PROOF 65mm. 5ozs. 925 Ag plate
	£25		Battle of Trafalgar	Au		200th. Anniversary Nelson.	PROOF .916 Au 7.98gms. 22mm.
	£5		End of War	Cu-Ni		Returning Evacuees	unc.
	£5		End of War	Ag		Returning Evacuees	PROOF .925 Ag
	£5		End of War	Au	150	Returning Evacuees	PROOF .916 Au 39.94 gms. 38.6m
	£5		End of War	Cu-Ni		Searchlights+Big Ben	unc.
	£5		End of War	Ag		Searchlights+Big Ben	PROOF 925 Ag
	£5		End of War	Au	low	Searchlights+Big Ben	PROOF .916 Au 39.94 gms. 38.6m
	£10		End of War	Ag		Searchlights+Big Ben	PROOF 5 ozs. 925 Ag 65mm.
2006	1p	X	currency	Cu/Steel	585,000	Le Hocq	
	2p	X	currency	Cu/Steel	1,200,000	Dolmen	
	5p	X	currency	Cu-Ni	1,200,000	Seymour Tower	
	10p	X	currency	Cu-Ni		L'Hermitage	
	20p	X	currency	Cu-Ni	500,000	Corbiere Lighthouse	
	50p	X	currency	Cu-Ni	300,000	Grosnez Castle	
	£1	X	currency	Ni-Brass		"Resolute"	
	£2	X	currency	Br / Cu-Ni		Parish Emblems	outer Nickel- Brass /Inner circle Cu-N
	£5		Great Britons Series	Cu-Ni		Sir Winston Churchill	unc.
	£5		Great Britons Series	Ag	25,000	Sir Winston Churchill	PROOF .925 Ag
	£5		Great Britons Series	Au	low	Sir Winston Churchill	PROOF .916 Au 39.94 gms. 38.6m
	£5		Great Britons Series	Cu-Ni		Charles Darwin	unc.
	£5		Great Britons Series	Ag	25,000	Charles Darwin	PROOF .925 Ag
	£5		Great Britons Series	Au	low	Charles Darwin	PROOF .916 Au 39.94 gms. 38.6m
	£5		Great Britons Series	Cu-Ni		Bobby Moore	unc.
	£5		Great Britons Series	Ag		Bobby Moore	PROOF .925 Ag

£5		Great Britons Series	Au	low	Bobby Moore	PROOF .916 Au 39.94gms. 38.6mm
£5		Great Britons Series	Cu-Ni		Florence Nightingale	unc.
£5		Great Britons Series	Ag		Florence Nightingale	PROOF 925 Ag
£5		Great Britons Series	Au	low	Florence Nightingale	PROOF .916 Au 39.94gms. 38.6mm
£5		Great Britons Series	Cu-Ni		Queen Mother	unc.
£5		Great Britons Series	Ag		Queen Mother	PROOF .925 Ag
£5		Great Britons Series	Au	low	Queen Mother	PROOF .916 Au 39.94gms. 38.6mm
£5		Great Britons Series	Cu-Ni		Henry V111	unc.
£5		Great Britons Series	Ag		Henry V111	PROOF .925 Ag
£5		Great Britons Series	Au	low	Henry V111	PROOF .916 Au 39.94gms. 38.6mm
£5		Great Britons Series	Cu-Ni		Princess Diana	unc.
£5		Great Britons Series	Ag	25,000	Princess Diana	PROOF .925 Ag
£5		Great Britons Series	Au	low	Princess Diana	PROOF .916 Au 39.94gms. 38.6mm
£5		Great Britons Series	Cu-Ni		Sir Christopher Wren	unc.
£5		Great Britons Series	Ag		Sir Christopher Wren	PROOF .925 Ag
£5		Great Britons Series	Au	low	Sir Christopher Wren	PROOF .916 Au 39.94gms. 38.6mm
£5		H.M.Queen 80th. Birthday	Cu-Ni		Head above streamers+date.	unc.
£5		H.M.Queen 80th. Birthday	Ag		Head above streamers+date.	PROOF gold cameo .925 Ag
£5		H.M.Queen 80th. Birthday	Au	low	Head above streamers+date.	PROOF .916 Au 39.94gms. 38.6mm
£5		H.M.Queen 80th. Birthday	Cu-Ni		Trooping the colour	unc.
£5		H.M.Queen 80th. Birthday	Cu-Ni		Trooping the colour	PROOF
£5		H.M.Queen 80th. Birthday	Ag		Trooping the colour	PROOF
£5		H.M.Queen 80th. Birthday	Ag		Trooping the colour	PROOF gold cameo .925 Ag
£5		H.M.Queen 80th. Birthday	Au	low	Trooping the colour	PROOF .916 Au 39.94gms. 38.6mm
£5		H.M.Queen 80th. Birthday	Cu-Ni		H.M. Queen and Wembley Stadium	unc.
£5		H.M.Queen 80th. Birthday	Ag		H.M. Queen and Wembley Stadium	PROOF gold cameo .925 Ag
£5		H.M.Queen 80th. Birthday	Au	low	H.M. Queen and Wembley Stadium	PROOF .916 Au 39.94gms. 38.6mm
£5		Victoria Cross Winners	Cu-Ni		Guy Gibson unc.	
£5		Victoria Cross Winners	Ag		Guy Gibson PROOF	.925 Ag
£5		Victoria Cross Winners	Au	low	Guy Gibson PROOF	.916 Au 39.94gms. 38.6mm
£5		Victoria Cross Winners	Cu-Ni		Eric James Nicolson	unc.
£5		Victoria Cross Winners	Ag		Eric James Nicolson	PROOF .925 Ag
£5		Victoria Cross Winners	Au		Eric James Nicolson	PROOF .916 Au 39.94gms. 38.6mm
£5		Victoria Cross Winners	Cu-Ni		Hook,Chard and Bromhead	unc.
£5		Victoria Cross Winners	Ag		Hook,Chard and Bromhead	PROOF .925 Ag
£5		Victoria Cross Winners	Au	low	Hook,Chard and Bromhead	PROOF .916 Au 39.94gms. 38.6mm
£5		Victoria Cross Winners	Cu-Ni		1st. Lancs Fusiliers	unc.
£5		Victoria Cross Winners	Ag		1st. Lancs Fusiliers	PROOF .925 Ag
£5		Victoria Cross Winners	Au	low	1st. Lancs Fusiliers	PROOF .916 Au 39.94gms. 38.6mm
£5		Victoria Cross Winners	Cu-Ni		Noel Chavasse	unc.
£5		Victoria Cross Winners	Ag		Noel Chavasse	PROOF .925 Ag
£5		Victoria Cross Winners	Au	low	Noel Chavasse	PROOF .916 Au 39.94gms. 38.6mm
£5		Victoria Cross Winners	Cu-Ni		David Mackay　Lucknow, 1857	unc.
£5		Victoria Cross Winners	Ag		David Mackay　Lucknow, 1857	PROOF .925 Ag
£5		Victoria Cross Winners	Au	low	David Mackay　Lucknow, 1857	PROOF .916 Au 39.94gms. 38.6mm
£5		Train Series- Gilt Finish	Ag		Coronation Scot	PROOF .925 Ag
£5		Train Series- Gilt Finish	Ag		Flying Scotsman	PROOF .925 Ag
£5		Train Series- Gilt Finish	Ag		Fireman and Driver	PROOF .925 Ag
£5		Train Series- Gilt Finish	Ag		Box Tunnel PROOF	.925 Ag
2007	10p	X	currency	Cu-Ni	630,000	L'Hermitage	
	20p	X	currency	Cu-Ni	780,000	La Corbiere	
	£1		Diana Commem.	Au	5,000	Diana - "The work continues"	PROOF .916 Au 9mm. 1.24 gms.
	£2	X	currency	NiBr/ Cu-Ni		Parish Emblems	outer Nickel-Brass/Inner circle Cu-Ni
	£5		Diamond Wedding	Cu-Ni		Balcony Scene Waving. unc.	
	£5		Diamond Wedding	Ag		Balcony Scene Waving.	PROOF .925 Ag
	£10		Diamond Wedding	Pt	low	Balcony Scene Waving.	PROOF 38.6mm (1st platinum coin)
	£5		Diamond Wedding	Cu-Ni		Wedding Cake	unc.
	£5		Diamond Wedding	Ag		Wedding Cake	PROOF .925 Ag
	£5		Diamond Wedding	Cu-Ni		H.M.Queen and H.R.H. Prince Philip	unc.

£5		Diamond Wedding	Ag		H.M.Queen and H.R.H. Prince Philip	PROOF .925 Ag	
£5		Diamond Wedding	Cu-Ni		Arrival at Abbey.	unc.	
£5		Diamond Wedding	Ag		Arrival at Abbey.	PROOF .925 Ag	
£5		Diamond Wedding	Au	low	Arrival at Abbey.	PROOF .916 Au 39.94gms. 38.6m	
2008	1p	X	currency	Cu/Steel	4,800,000	Le Hocq	
	2p	X	currency	Cu/Steel	2,400,000	Dolmen	
	5p	X	currency	Cu-Ni	3,600,000	Seymour Tower	
	£5		Commemmorative	Ag		George+Dragon	PROOF frosted .925 Ag 26mm. 8gm
	£5		History of RAF	Cu-Ni		Dambusters, Wallis,Chadwick,Gibson.	Barnes Wallis/ Roy Chadwick/Guy Gibs
	£5		History of RAF	Ag / Cu	25,000	Dambusters, Wallis,Chadwick,Gibson.	PROOF Ag plated Copper
	£5		History of RAF	Ag		Dambusters, Wallis,Chadwick,Gibson.	PROOF .925 Ag 38.6mm
	£5		History of RAF	Cu-Ni		Frank Whittle	unc.
	£5		History of RAF	Ag	25,000	Frank Whittle	PROOF .925 Ag 38.6mm
	£5		History of RAF	Au	low	Frank Whittle	PROOF .916 Au 39.94gms. 38.6m
	£5		History of RAF	Cu-Ni		R.J.Mitchell unc.	
	£5		History of RAF	Ag	25,000	R.J.Mitchell	PROOF .925 Ag 38.6 mm
	£5		History of RAF	Au	low	R.J.Mitchell	PROOF .916 Au 39.94 gms. 38.6m
	£10		History of RAF	Ag		R.J.Mitchell	PROOF 65mm. 5ozs .925 Ag
	£10		History of RAF	Au / Ag		R.J.Mitchell	PROOF 65 mm. 5ozs .925 Ag/ Au plate
	£5		Formation of R.A.F.	Cu-Ni		Maj. Gen. Sir Hugh Trenchard	unc. (Trenchard was founder of RA
	£5		Formation of R.A.F.	Ag	25,000	Maj. Gen. Sir Hugh Trenchard	PROOF .925 Ag
	£5		Formation of R.A.F.	Au	low	Maj. Gen. Sir Hugh Trenchard	PROOF .916 Au 39.94gms. 38.6m
	£5		Formation of R.A.F.	Cu-Ni		Bomber Command	unc.
	£5		Formation of R.A.F.	Ag	25,000	Bomber Command	PROOF .925 Ag
	£5		Formation of R.A.F.	Au	low	Bomber Command	PROOF .916 Au 39.94gms. 38.6m
	£5		Formation of R.A.F.	Cu-Ni		Coastal Command	unc.
	£5		Formation of R.A.F.	Ag	25,000	Coastal Command	PROOF .925 Ag
	£5		Formation of R.A.F.	Au	low	Coastal Command	PROOF .916 Au 39.94gms. 38.6m
	£5		Formation of R.A.F.	Cu-Ni		Fighter Command	unc.
	£5		Formation of R.A.F.	Ag	25,000	Fighter Command	PROOF .925 Ag
	£5		Formation of R.A.F.	Au		Fighter Command	PROOF .916 Au 39.94gms. 38.6m
	£5		Battle of Britain	Cu-Ni			unc.
	£5		Battle of Britain	Ag			PROOF .925 Ag
	£5		Battle of Britain	Au			PROOF .916 Au 39.94gms. 38.6m
	£5		Poppy-Royal British Legion	Cu-Ni		Poppy with circular "Lest we forget"	Poppy shape, polished die, Ht=38.6m
	£5		Poppy-Royal British Legion	Ag	9,500	Poppy with circular "Lest we forget"	PROOF Poppy shape .925 Ag 38.6m
	£5		Poppy-Royal British Legion	Au	450	Poppy with circular "Lest we forget"	PROOF Poppy shape .916 Au 38.6m
	£5		Flying Aces Series	Cu-Ni		Flying Legends	unc.
	£5		Flying Aces Series	Ag		Flying Legends	PROOF .925 Ag
	£5		Flying Aces Series	Au	low	Flying Legends	PROOF .916 Au 39.94gms. 38.6m
2009	20p	X	currency	Cu-Ni	1,500,000	La Corbiere	
	50p	X	currency	Cu-Ni	480,000	Grosnez	
	£5			Ag		George + Dragon	PROOF frosted .925 Ag 26mm.
	£5		Famous Battles	Ag	25,000	Battle of Agincourt	PROOF frosted .925 Ag 38.6mm
	£5		Famous Battles	Ag	25,000	Battle of the Somme	PROOF frosted .925 Ag 38.6mm
	£5		Capt.James Cook comm.	Ag	950	Capt. Cook + ship "Endeavour"	PROOF .925 Ag 38.6mm
	£5		Henry V111	Ag	950	500 th. Anniversary of Accession	PROOF .925 Ag 38.6mm
	£25		Henry V111	Au	450	500 th. Anniversary of Accession	PROOF .916 Au 22mm

VI MISCELLANEOUS

Jettons

During the Middle Ages all calculations that were not able to be performed as mental arithmetic were made in Roman figures as Arabic numerals were not generally in use in Northern Europe before the early part of the seventeenth century.

The maths was done by using counters on a chequered counting board usually on a rectangular tabletop. It is from this now defunct pastime that the name "Chancellor of the Exchequer" was derived, ie keeper of the chequerboard for the monarch.

The counters were thrown on to the lines and spaces on this board and a skilled user could perform additions and subtraction functions quite rapidly. The name "jetton" is from the French, meaning to throw.

In the early mediaeval period most jettons were made in England and the writer is unaware of any found in Jersey.

Around 1400 France became the centre of manufacture of these counters. There are many types, usually in bronze or brass, some with legends. A few have been found locally, the most common depicting a crown on the obverse with a legend AVE MARIA (Hail Mary) and some type of ornamental cross on the reverse.

France AE Jetton 27mm.
Second half XV century
diam. 27mm

France AE Heater-shield jetton.
15th century
diam. 30mm

Much more frequently encountered are jettons from the 16th century from Nuremberg in Germany, which became an important trading place, gradually taking over from France as the centre of production.

Germany Nuremberg AE Jetton
Early XVII century
diam. 25mm

These jettons are extremely common and are sometimes found in Jersey in house clearances. They are made of very thin brass and show the manufacturer's name, eg HANS KRAUWINCKEL and NUREMBURG spelt or abbreviated in different ways. The commonest type has on the obverse a design of three crowns and three fleurs de lys arranged in a circle around a rose. The reverse shows a crowned orb known as REICHSAPFEL. This is the arms of Nuremberg and there is a legend, usually in German, and of a religious significance.

Of course, whilst the use of these counters was intended as counting pieces, as elsewhere in Europe when the vast majority of the population was illiterate, they could possibly have been used as money by the poor for low value transactions in places such as markets.

Tokens

There is a vast series of 17th century tokens that appeared in England after the Civil War because the government there was unable or unwilling to accept the need to issue official copper to be used as small change. Many traders of all descriptions issued their own types of tokens, usually valued at a halfpenny or a farthing to satisfy the demand. Of course, these normally showed details of the issuers' name or business.

Unfortunately, it has be said that no Jersey token of this series has ever come to light so at present it is assumed that the imported French coppers into the Island adequately fulfilled local needs.

There were further issues of copper tokens during the 18th and 19th centuries on the mainland of penny, halfpenny and farthing value. It is thought that possibly up to a dozen circulated here. There are two tokens of this series with a local reference.

The first is dated 1812 on the obverse and has the legend JERSEY BANK TOKEN around a laureate head of George III right. The reverse shows A BANK OF ENGLAND NOTE FOR 240 TOKENS around ELIAS NEEL JERSEY.

The second, dated 1813, has on the obverse the legend JERSEY BANK around a draped and laureate bust right of George III. The reverse depicts a figure similar to Britannia seated left on a bale holding a pair of scales and a cornucopia with a ship in the distance with the legend ONE PENNY TOKEN.

Both of these tokens are extremely rare and thought possibly to have been patterns and not circulated.

It is worth reporting that a bronze farthing token issued by the Bristol Patent Sheathing & Nailing Co (reference Bell. Gloss. 9) has turned up here as frequently as all the other token discoveries of the 18th and 19th centuries put together.

It seems as if these tokens were deliberately imported into Jersey, perhaps around 1820 when these ceased to be legal tender in England. This would also indicate increasing readiness of the population to accept English money as opposed to French because of the Napoleonic war and the change in the French currency which was no longer based on the Tournois system that was familiar to the local population.

It should be pointed out that during the late 19th and early 20th centuries a number of local businesses issued tokens, the most common being of 1½ pence in value. These were from public houses, hotels and other merchants or tradesmen. Of course, it goes without saying that each token showed the name of the business and value could only be obtained in that particular establishment as no-one else would usually take it in payment. This is similar to the situation that existed with the private tokens in the 17th century in England, referred to earlier.

All diam. c. 25mm

It is worth noting that Jersey issued its first telephone card in June 1988 and has brought out regular releases until the last in March 2001. This is, in effect, a modern type of token. Both mint and used cards are sought after by collectors worldwide.

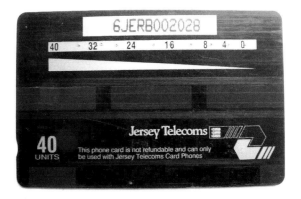

VIII THE GERMAN OCCUPATION, 1940-45

The German occupation commenced on 1st July 1940 and lasted until 9th May 1945.

Although a pound was worth 5 Reichsmark (RM) on 1st July, it was devalued to 8RM on 8th July and then revalued shortly after to 7RM, which was two shillings and ten pence halfpenny. The States of Jersey published an official pocket-sized exchange rate table, as it was quite difficult for the local population to calculate the correct amount of money on conversion. On 3rd September 1940 the pound was further devalued to 9.60RM.

The Germans flooded the Island with the Reichskreditkassenscheine notes which were only used in occupied countries in denominations of 50, 20, 5, 2 and 1RM, and also a 50 Reichspfennig note (see page 41). In practice, these were worth only the paper they were printed on and, as good money drives out bad, English coins slowly disappeared. A great amount was hoarded, whilst some were taken out of the Island by the occupying forces as souvenirs.

There followed a period where the following currency circulated:

> The Reichskredit marks referred to above
> 20 RM official notes as used in Germany
> German coins minted from the end of the First World War to date
> English notes and coins
> Guernsey notes and coins
> Jersey coins
> French notes and coins

There were no Jersey notes at first as recent issues did not exist, as was the case in Guernsey and England. The German 5 and 10 Pfennig coins (see page 40) were referred to by locals as 'washers' as the early ones had a hole punched in the centre.

Eventually, for daily usage there was a shortage of coin. As there was no metal available for minting purposes because of the War, in 1941 the States of Jersey launched a series of paper notes, the denominations being one pound, ten shillings, two shillings (2 types), one shilling and sixpence. These were engraved by the Jersey artist, Edmund Blampied, and printed locally. Despite this measure, eventually there were virtually only Marks left in circulation although shops still priced goods in £ s. d.

It is not surprising therefore that, despite further exchange rate alterations between the RM and the pound, barter became very common in all walks of life. For example, new clothing was unobtainable and the writer's late mother would repair and patch clothes (or make new ones out of pieces of material) for farmers and their families in exchange for farm produce. The local newspaper carried adverts every night from persons seeking to exchange goods or services.

After the Liberation, the Reichskreditmark notes were exchanged at the rate of £1 being equal to 9.36 RM. Gradually, all the other foreign coins were taken out of circulation, too, over the next few months.

When the Edmund Blampied notes were exchanged for current money, many people kept a sixpence, one or two shilling note as a souvenir so these are fairly readily available to collectors today. However, most of the ten shillings and one pound notes were handed in as, in 1945, these were considerable sums in terms of purchasing power. As a consequence, specimens of these two notes are quite difficult to obtain, especially in really good condition.

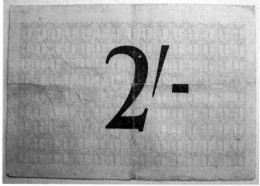

APPENDIX A

THE JERSEY COMMUNION TOKEN

Although strictly outside the scope of a book on coinage, it would seem that this para-numismatic item is of sufficient interest to mention.

It is in no way currency, being of no monetary value. It was the custom of Scottish churches to issue such tokens to intending communicants, giving them admission to the sacrament.

The "Scots Church" in Midvale Road, St Helier, issued tokens dated 1853 for this purpose. They should be considered as passes, and included numbers indicating at which table the holder should attend.

In 1853, the church was part of the Free Church of Scotland, although it is now part of the established Church of Scotland. The inscription "St Heliers Church" is misleading, as there is no connection with St Helier's Parish Church. The use of these tokens did not last very long, as they were replaced by Communion Cards. Few seem to have survived and they are thus quite rare.

It was customary for Communion Tokens to be struck in base metals such as lead, pewter, or white metal. The Jersey example was quite exceptional, as at least some were struck in silver.

References:

McCammon	C.141 J - C.143 J
Cresswell	3037
Burinski	3448

Creswell has also recorded a variety lacking the words *Nec tamen consumabatur* (No. 5635), but no examples are known locally.

Common obverse to all four

Width   26.5 mm
Height   20.0mm

APPENDIX B

FRÉLUQUES

Coins or tokens know as fréluques are mentioned in surviving records of the States of Guernsey dated 1535 and 1619, forbidding the manufacture and use of these unauthorised pieces.

It has long been a numismatic mystery as to the exact nature of these fréluques. Some small base metal pieces found in Guernsey are considered possible survivors of this enigmatic coinage, and it is understood that research is proceeding in this connection.

Two similar pieces have been found in Jersey, both at Gorey Castle. One is illustrated. There is no other evidence at present of extensive circulation in Jersey.

Central design: rose or rosette
Diameter of irregular flan approximately 10.00mm

APPENDIX C

THE GERMAN OCCUPATION 'TOKENS'

From time to time, tokens which seem to have been issued by the Germans during the period 1940-45 in the Channel Islands appear on the market or are brought to the Numismatics Section for identification. No such items were struck at the time – all were made in California, U.S.A., in the 1970s by a partnership of two men who produced other series of tokens (unconnected with the Channel Islands) as well.

A full list of these appears in *Currencies of the Anglo-Norman Isles ii* by A. L. T. McCammon (i.e. the supplement published in 1993) – pages 82 and 83. The whole range is reproduced photographically here so that collectors can compare any pieces with the pictures.

The items have the following in common:

(i)   all are uniface (i.e. blank reverse);
(ii)   they appear to be produced in a variety of base metals of copper, bronze, brass and also zinc;
(iii)   some of these have been chemically treated to artifically 'age' them.

Considerable numbers of all these items must have been produced as many have been seen, particularly in Europe and the U.S.A. (where they were purchased after production).

These pieces have now become 'collectables' in their own right but it should be stressed that in numismatics they are known as 'fantasy pieces'. Collectors should ensure that they only pay a small amount for these as there is a danger of never even getting your money back in the future if too high prices are paid; having said that, it is known that some numismatists do attempt to collect the series.

The purpose of this article is simply as a WARNING as the Numismatics Section has heard in recent years of a number of members of the public who have paid quite high prices for odd examples thinking that these are rare, genuine tokens and quite valuable. The author has seen varieties and examples in different metals not listed in McCammons.

The following examples are listed in the order of McCammon's listing referred to earlier:

	Reference	Metal	Diameter or height x length
	C121Cl	Brass	27.8mm
	C121Cl but scalloped edge – not in McCammon	Brass	27.8mm
	C122J this example copper – not in McCammon	Brass	38.9mm
	C123G (i)	Brass	27.7 x 39.5mm
	C123G (ii) Note kidney-shaped hole left	Zinc	27.7 x 39.5mm

Reference	Metal	Diameter or height x length

C129J | Brass | 35.4mm

C129J | Copper (as above – not in McCammon) | 35.4mm

C130J | Zinc | 63.45 x 33.25mm

C131CI (i) | Zinc | 39 - 64.7mm

NB C131CI (ii) not pictured – as above but small circles left and right are holes.

C132CI | Zinc | 38.8 - 64.7mm

	Reference	Metal	Diameter or height x length
	C124G	Zinc	32.35mm
	C125J	Brass	40.9mm (side)
	C126J	Brass	35.3mm
	C127J (i) this example copper – not in McCammon	Brass	35.3mm

NB C127J (ii) not pictured – as above but in place of star top left there is a square hole.

| | C128J | Brass | 35.3mm |

SELECT BIBLIOGRAPHY

The standard work for further reading is A. L. T. McCammon, *Currencies of the Anglo-Norman Isles* (London 1984) and the supplement (London 1993).

There has been copious literature on the Coriosolites and other Armorican coinage, but much of it is in French and some rather dated in the light of modern research. However, although originally published over sixty years ago in the *Bulletin of the Société Jersiaise* for 1937, N. V. L. Rybot's 'Armorican Art', with its splendid line drawings of the coins from the La Marquanderie Hoard, is essential for any study of this series. A much more recent work Philip de Jersey, *Coinage in Iron Age Armorica* (Oxford 1994) gives a detailed summary of not only the Coriosolite but also the other Armorican coinages which have occurred in Jersey hoards.

Other articles on this series are: D. Corbel & G. Gallichan, 'The Le Catillon Hoard acquisition'; and John Hooker, 'Notes on part of the Catillon Hoard purchased by the Société Jersiaise in 1989', published in the Société Jersiaise Annual Bulletins 1990 and 1993 respectively. The full result of John Hooker's investigations have been published in B.A.R. International Series.

For a general survey of Roman coinage, among many modern publications there is A. Burnett, *Coinage in the Roman World* (London 1987). See also R. W. Higginbottom, 'Roman Coin Finds in Jersey' (*Spinks Numismatic Circular*, February 1979). Other Seaby and Spink publications on the Roman series are always helpful.

Spink Standard Catalogue, *Coins of England and the United Kingdom*, is the best general reference for these coins; there is also Coincraft's *Standard Catalogue of English & UK Coins, 1066 to Date*.

Reference books on the French series are necessary in view of the significance of French currency in Jersey. For a long time, the standard work was L. Ciani, *Les Monnaies Royales Francais* (Paris 1926), but a much improved update of this book is J. Duplessey, *Les Monnaies Francaises Royales* (2 volumes, Paris 1988, 1989). Listings in both these works terminate at the end of the reign of Louis XVI. The most useful general survey of French coinage, in English, is N. Mayhew, *Coinage in France from the Dark Ages to Napoleon* (London 1988). Subsequent French issues, and "World Coins" are listed in the K-M publications. An invaluable little booklet, F.C. Higgins, *Copper Coins of Europe till 1892* (London 1892, reprinted 1970), is worthy of mention, as it covers most of the 'foreign' copper coinage that has turned up in Jersey.

For actual Jersey coinage, a standard work is F. Pridmore, *The British Commonwealth of Nations, Part I* (London 1960), covering issues, including tokens, up to the Liberation Penny of 1949. Seaby's *Coins of Scotland, Ireland and the Islands* lists issues up to 1981, but a more recent publication, Coincraft's *Standard Catalogue of the Coins of Scotland, Channel Islands & Isle of Man* lists Jersey coinage up to 1998, including the numerous special issues and proofs issued in recent years.

Some of the above publications are still in print, or can often be obtained from numismatic booksellers.

A very comprehensive bibliography concerning all series of coinage relating to Jersey will be found in McCammon's *Currencies of the Anglo-Norman Isles*, pp 349-358.